# Beyond the Half-Way Covenant

# Beyond the Half-Way Covenant

Solomon Stoddard's Understanding
of the Lord's Supper as a Converting Ordinance

David Paul McDowell

WIPF & STOCK · Eugene, Oregon

BEYOND THE HALF-WAY COVENANT
Solomon Stoddard's Understanding of the Lord's Supper as a Converting Ordinance

Wipf & Stock
An Imprint of Wipf and Stock Publishers
199 W. 8th Ave., Suite 3
Eugene, OR 97401
www.wipfandstock.com

ISBN 13: 978-1-61097-976-4
Manufactured in the U.S.A.

I would like to dedicate this book to two very special congregations that I have served while I have been working toward my doctorate, writing my dissertation, and completing this book. I dedicate this work to College Church, Northampton, MA, where I served for twenty-five years and first learned about Solomon Stoddard. I also dedicate this work to Community Fellowship Church, West Chicago, IL, where I am in my seventh year of serving as Senior Pastor. Both of these congregations are filled with wonderful examples of a warm and engaging evangelical faith that is unafraid to live out the gospel and be the hands and feet of Jesus in this broken world.

# Contents

# Foreword

THE READER OF *Beyond the Half-Way Covenant* is entitled to ask, "What difference does a debate about the Lord's Supper and church polity, rooted in early 18th century New England theology, make in the church today?" Isn't this just a debate about something that has no relevance to the American church in the 21st century? I confess, even though I had studied this controversy, I wondered this myself when I began to read this new book. My question was soon answered by David McDowell's historically rich, and pastorally insightful, analysis.

Here you meet one of America's most powerful, indeed colorful, early preachers. Solomon Stoddard would be a household name, even a mega-church pastor, if he were living in our modern Protestant world. But because of his own conversion experience, which came through the means of the Lord's Supper, he held unique views on Communion and salvation. You will understand these views by reading McDowell's work. But Stoddard's view of Communion was not merely argued from his personal experience! Like all well-trained pastors of his time, and most were rigorously well-trained, Stoddard had studied both English Puritanism and Scottish Presbyterianism. His oft-maligned Communion views are critically examined by McDowell in their proper Puritan context. They are also examined in terms of their impact on pastoral life in early America. This is part of the reason why this book matters to us today.

Like most students of early American church history and pastoral practice what I knew about Solomon Stoddard, and particularly about the controversy over Communion and regeneration, was shaped by what I knew about his famous grandson, Jonathan Edwards. I knew that Edwards had succeeded his grandfather as pastor of the Congregational Church in Northampton. I knew that Edwards eventually opposed his grandfather's views on Communion. I knew that this stance contributed directly to Edwards being dismissed by the congregation after an amazing time in our national history that has been called *The Great*

*Awakening*. I also knew that before The Great Awakening Stoddard had presided over seasons of revival, or great "harvests." There were at least five (or maybe six) of these times of revival. By anyone's standards this was a remarkably fruitful leader regardless of his (misunderstood) views about Communion and salvation.

Personally, I thought I had understood Stoddard's position and importance by reading Edwards and the work of Edwards' biographers. But I was clearly wrong in this assumption. This is precisely where McDowell has done us a great service. He has carefully studied the sermons and written effects of Solomon Stoddard and allowed him to now be heard on his own terms. And those terms are both interesting and important. They even have some things to say to modern leaders and churches if they will listen to the past with an open mind and heart.

This thought-provoking book further provides the kind of historical context that allows the reader to grasp the theology and practice of some of our earliest American Protestant ministers. It reveals how deeply divided these leaders were and how their respective churches suffered under the weight of controversy. In this sense nothing is really new under the sun. We still suffer under the influence of ministers and controversies related to their teaching and practice. We may have little or no understanding of these particular issues today but by reading this fine book you will gain more understanding of past conflicts, which could help you in dealing better with current ones.

You will also learn how seriously these ministers and churches took theology, something we have too little time for in the modern age. We further learn how the force of human personality always plays a major role in church controversy. People think that Jonathan Edwards, who still attracts considerable interest as an American religious thinker, cast Stoddard in a negative light. For this reason most modern readers have done the same. But Solomon Stoddard was a magnificent man, a great preacher (better by far than his famous grandson) and a true pioneer for Christian mission in a time when the church did not yet grasp the importance of how to reach people who were outside the grace of God experientially yet visibly joined to the local congregation.

So, why should *you* read this book? You should read it because it will help you understand how history has been written and stories badly told. Very often historians and biographers have placed their stress on the more prominent names and figures of an era rather than by digging into the original source material itself. McDowell takes you to the source material and thus gives you new insights into a great Christian man. He also reveals some things about controversies and controversialists that would help us do a much better job of sorting out our own differences in modern churches. We need rigorous minds joined with tender and loving hearts. In Stoddard we can see something of these two in one person, and a person who has so often been misunderstood.

I am thrilled to see the record about Stoddard corrected. I like the way this story is simply told. I thus commend this book to Christian leaders who want a better grasp of the past, a deeper sense of the problems of pastoral controversy, and real fuel for a deep longing for true revival.

Dr. John H. Armstrong
President, ACT 3
Carol Stream, Illinois
Author, *Your Church Is Too Small:*
*Why Unity in Christ's Mission Is Vital*
*to the Future of the Church*

# Preface

THIS BOOK IS BASED upon my doctoral dissertation examining the influence and unique views of Solomon Stoddard (1643–1729), the grandfather of Jonathan Edwards and the second pastor of the church in Northampton, Massachusetts. His views of the Lord's Supper and church polity were considered to be controversial innovations by many Congregationalists. Increase Mather and Edward Taylor in particular believed that he profoundly deviated from the Puritan Founders and was a threat the future of the New England Way, i.e., a system of governance based upon the voluntary commitment (covenant) of its citizens to be ruled on a local level religiously and politically under the authority of the Bible. This system developed into Congregationalism with its emphasis of belonging to a local church within a particular community.

Using archival printed primary and secondary material, as well as trying to read his microscopic handwriting, I have tried to demonstrate three things: First, Stoddard's views can only be understood within the wider context of the decline of Puritanism and the liberalizing force of the Half-Way Covenant; Second, Stoddard's view of Communion and polity grew out of his own study of English Puritanism and Scottish Presbyterianism, as well as his own conversion experience at the Lord's Table, and, far from being a corrupting influence on the church in Northampton, became the very context for evangelical revival leading to five (or six) separate "harvests" in his nearly sixty years of ministry; and Third, while Stoddard's view of Communion had an immediate impact on Northampton and the future ministry of Jonathan Edwards, it also had a wider influence on a significant number of churches in the Connecticut Valley.

Since most of the scholarly work done on Stoddard thus far has come as an appendage to Edwards studies, future work focusing on Stoddard awaits the labor of willing minds. This book is written, therefore, in the hope that it may encourage further research on this most fascinating man.

David Paul McDowell
West Chicago, IL

# Acknowledgments

I WOULD LIKE TO acknowledge my wife Gloria for her support and significant help in editing both my dissertation and the manuscript for this book. I would also like to thank the research librarians at the Forbes Library, Northampton, MA, for their helpful assistance in providing time and material for my study. I want to acknowledge my debt to Dr. Richard Lovelace for initially giving me the idea of writing my dissertation on the life of Solomon Stoddard, and to Dr. Ronald Clutter and Dr. Robert Clouse for their encouragement to turn my dissertation into a book. I greatly appreciate my friend John Armstrong and his suggestion to send my book proposal to Wipf & Stock, and the opportunity the latter has given me to publish this work to reach a larger audience.

## Stoddard Solomon

Pastor of the church of Northampton Mass, has been always considered as one of the greatest divines of New England, He was born in Boston, in 1643 & & was graduated at Harvard College, in 1662. He was afterwards appointed a fellow His health having been impaired, by a close application to his Studies, he went to Barbados as Chaplain to Governour Serle, & preached with great acceptance to the dissenters on that island, near 2 years On his return being ordained Sept 11 1672, as successor to Mr Mather at Northampton, he continued in that place till his death Feb 11 1729 in the 86th year of his age,

# Introduction

ELEAZER MATHER WAS MARRIED to Esther Warham on September 29, 1659, in Windsor, Connecticut. They both hailed from very significant families in Puritan New England. He was the son of Richard Mather of Dorchester, MA, the brother of Increase Mather, and the uncle of Cotton Mather; and she the daughter of the famous John Warham of Windsor. Before their marriage, Eleazer came to Northampton, Massachusetts, in July 1658 as the town's first pastor and was subsequently ordained in the church at Northampton on June 18, 1661.[1] There was hope that the son of the famous minister from Dorchester might attract more people to the fledgling town. However, his ministry was turbulent and short-lived and about the time he lay dying, a young graduate of Harvard's class of 1662 returned to Boston from the Barbados, where he had retreated in 1667 for health reasons and to preach to Congregationalists living there. This young man was Solomon Stoddard, who was born in Boston in September 1643. He was one of fifteen sons born to a wealthy Boston merchant, Anthony Stoddard. Solomon's mother was Mary Downing, Anthony's second wife and a niece of Governor John Winthrop.

Solomon Stoddard's bags were already packed and stowed aboard ship in the Boston harbor. Stoddard was headed for a new ministry opportunity in London when he was intercepted by a search committee of five men from the town of Northampton on the western edge of the Massachusetts Bay Colony. Ruling elder John Strong was no Guillame Farel and Stoddard no John Calvin, but the situation bore a vague resemblance to the famous interdiction of the Reformer and his consequent long-term pastorate in Geneva. Stoddard accepted the offer to preach in Northampton and was called to be its second pastor in March 1670. He responded to the call by saying, "Sirs, I accept your offer. And I promise

1. Unless otherwise noted, facts concerning Stoddard in Northampton are from James R. Trumbull, *The History of Northampton from its Settlement in 1654*. Thanks to the research librarians at Forbes Library, Northampton, MA, for making this and other original documents available.

to give myself and the residue of my days to the service of the House of God in your town."[2] And give himself he did, more than doubling Calvin's years in Geneva and bringing to Northampton an influence and legacy to which his grandson Jonathan Edwards constantly referred.

Northampton was on the frontier, but not so far from Boston to be out of reach of the Half-Way Covenant controversy. The Half-Way Covenant of 1662 tried to address the problem that many of the second generation Puritan adults experienced. Although they were baptized as infants, many could not give testimony to their personal regeneration and yet wanted their children baptized. The Synod of 1662 mandated that these parents could substitute a confession of faith (called "owning the covenant") for a personal testimony of saving grace. This confession would earn for them a type of membership which would give them the privilege of baptizing their children, but not of participating in the Lord's Supper.

Eleazer Mather was against this "liberalizing" measure and was a supporter of the Cambridge Platform of 1648, which drew a sharp distinction between full regenerate members (those in the state of grace) and those who were unregenerate albeit "professing Christians." It was John Cotton, who in 1634 "had institutionalized a test for regenerate church membership in new Boston and made it the basis of civil enfranchisement."[3]

Mather's strict Congregationalism was not universally accepted and a more moderate Puritanism characterized the Connecticut River Valley. In reality, many of the river towns in Massachusetts were populated by former residents of Connecticut and had been greatly influenced by the perspective of Thomas Hooker. Hooker believed that "civil enfranchisement," i.e., the right to vote, should be disconnected from church membership, thus bringing equality between the non-churched members of the town and the members of the town's church. The practice of connecting the two did not produce harmony, especially in towns like Hartford, Wethersfield, Windsor, and Stratford, but it did explain why the Half-Way Covenant generally gained strong support within the Connecticut colony. "Enlarged baptism dominated the churches of Connecticut by 1690. Of the churches whose adoption of the Half-Way Covenant we can date, seventy per cent made the change by the end

2. W. Stoddard, "A Liberal Among the Puritans," 33.
3. Coffman, *Solomon Stoddard*, 28.

of 1671."[4] Non-members saw the Half-Way Covenant as a measure of enhancing their independence from ecclesiastical authority.

> Non-members, eager to weaken the bastion of the autonomous church, adopted the covenant and used it to broaden and dilute ecclesiastical authority, and narrow the distance between the church and the community. Their numbers and influence proved sufficient to alter the covenant destiny of Connecticut. As the formerly stymied lay and clerical adherents of extended baptism received the potent support of the unregenerates, the covenant gradually developed sufficient momentum to carry it over the opposition in a number of towns in the colony.[5]

The original impetus for the Half-Way Covenant grew out of the church's fear of losing the second and third generations of the Puritan commonwealth. The children and grandchildren of the "visible saints," while mostly professing Christians and morally upright, could not point to an experience of saving grace, which was the hallmark of John Cotton's "code."[6] "Of professing Christians there was no lack, but many were not qualifying for full membership even though it brought both access to the Lord's Table and the right to bring children to baptism."[7]

Therefore, the Synod of 1662 established "half-way" measures, which stated that the children of baptized members were to be declared members under care of the church although they were not allowed access to the Lord's Supper or the vote. In addition, these baptized children, upon remaining unconverted as adults and presenting their own children for baptism, had to renew allegiance to the covenant by professing faith in Christ. This would still not qualify them for full membership with the right to take the Lord's Supper, but it would seal their offspring to the church through baptism. The hope was that inclusion of

4. Pope, *The Half-Way Covenant*, 124–125.

5. Lucas, *Valley of Discord*, 78.

6. "Cotton's 'code,' also referred to as *Moses His Judicials*, was a document of ten chapters which represented a major departure from English common law. Its heavy reliance upon Scripture provides an important illustration of the strong religious influence which infused Puritan thinking about law and administration. . . . Although, for reasons that are unclear, this code was never enacted into law, it formed the basis for the codes adopted by the colonies of New Haven and Southampton and served as the prototype for the codes that were finally adopted by the Colony." McClendon, "Puritan Jurisprudence," para. 21.

7. Ahlstrom, *A Religious History*, 159.

the unregenerate children of the covenant would lead to their eventual conversion. The Half-Way Covenant, however, did not yield the desired outcome, but instead created a two-tiered system of membership as well as a bifurcation of the sacraments. As a result, the Lord's Supper (not baptism) became the unique privilege of the converted, whereas baptism (not the Lord's Supper) became a right by birth into the church. Richard Mather summed up this division: "It is one thing to be in the Covenant and in the Church, in respect of external state, and another thing to enjoy all the spiritual and external benefits of such a relation; and though this latter be the portion of none but such as come to be truly regenerate, yet the other is, and so continues, the right of all that have once had it."[8]

Historian Perry Miller accuses the Puritans of hypocrisy in these half-way measures.[9] He claims that the apologists for the Half-Way Covenant used the analogy of circumcision (Gen 17) to defend their view of baptism. Miller identifies the inherent weakness of this argument by pointing out that the church was not a nation and such an analogy only tended to sacrifice the spiritual and internal for the ritual and external. The Puritans, therefore, drifted back into the same externalism from which they had originally separated themselves and in that, so Miller claims, was their hypocrisy.

It has already been mentioned that Eleazer Mather was opposed to these half-way measures. His opposition was not only a surprise to the congregation at Northampton, but it was doomed to failure from the start. In addition, he stirred up controversy by making his coming to Northampton contingent upon the acquisition of some of the town's best land.[10] The requested land was not for him alone, but also for several families that he wanted to bring with him from Dorchester. In spite of the controversy, however, the town was so eager to have a pastor that it granted his request and decided that each citizen would make a donation of land for this purpose.

The town's support for Mather continued to erode when he, supported by the families from Dorchester, decided to apply Cotton's "code"

8. Miller, *The New England Mind*, 98.

9. The reader should note Miller's discussion of Puritan hypocrisy in chapter 5 of *The New England Mind*.

10. Lucas, 84. Edward Elmer led the opposition, which was not so much centered on Mather as on a general dissatisfaction with town government. Mather's land grant became part of this overall issue.

and require a satisfactory description of one's regenerative experience to the minister as a requirement for membership, just the opposite direction of the half-way measures. Active opposition to his ministry grew fierce when "he blocked the desires of some members and many non-members to adopt the Half-Way Covenant. Aware of the difficulties the town had experienced in its search for a minister, Mather gave it a choice of either having the covenant or himself."[11]

There is little evidence that Eleazer Mather had a happy life in what is now called "Happy Valley" by its inhabitants. He wrote nothing to be published, and if it were not for his brother Increase, we would have no first-hand record of his preaching. Increase gathered and published some of Eleazer's sermons in a pamphlet called *A Serious Exhortation to the Present and Succeeding Generations in New England* (1671). The sermons read like a jeremiad and manifested great discouragement owing to a combination of church/town controversies and physical ailments. Eleazer became seriously ill in 1667 and could not continue to lead the charge against the supporters of the Half-Way Covenant, which by this time comprised the majority of the town. In fact, the controversy was so rancorous that the town presented its petition for the Half-Way Covenant to their minister when poor Mather was on his deathbed. The church in Northampton petitioned for the half-way measures in the spring of 1669, just before his death on July 24.

> Such amongst us, being settled inhabitants that give us ground to hope in charity that there may be some good thing in them towards the Lord tho' in the lowest degree, understanding and believing the doctrine of faith . . . and freely professing their assent unto not being scandalous in life and so solemnly taking hold of the covenant, may have their children baptized and entered. Also the adult children hitherto unbaptized, of confederate believers, without themselves coming up to aforesaid qualifications, may be accepted members and themselves baptized.[12]

It was during this time frame that the search committee from the town went to Boston to search for Mather's successor as was previously mentioned.[13] They found Solomon Stoddard, who was about as unlike

---

11. Ibid.

12. Coffman, 58.

13. Lucas, 85. Lucas emphasizes that the town's victory over the church lay not only in adopting extended baptism and the "state of education," but in gaining the right to

Eleazer Mather as one could imagine. Stoddard agreed to a trial period of approximately three months, after which he began his duties in Northampton on March 4, 1670. On March 18, 1670, Stoddard married Esther, Eleazer Mather's widow.[14] This was neither odd nor scandalous, but part of an accepted practice when calling a young single pastor to a town where there was a young widowed pastor's wife already living in the parsonage.

> In the forthright New England of the seventeenth century there was a method in such situations so frequently observed that it might almost be called a custom. When a minister died, after a town had invested in him to the extent of land and a house, and the widow was of marriageable age, they summoned a young bachelor to the pulpit. A few months after Eleazar's death, Solomon Stoddard, eight years out of Harvard, came by invitation to exhibit a sample of his preaching; on March 18, 1670, he married Esther Mather.[15]

Oddly, for reasons yet to be discussed, Stoddard waited to be ordained for a period of two years. Finally, on September 11, 1672, he was ordained as the second minister of the church at the hands of Mr. John Strong, ruling elder of the church at Northampton and Mr. John Whiting, pastor of the Second Church in Hartford.[16]

The moderate Congregationalists of Northampton knew that their new pastor would implement the provisions of the Half-Way Covenant

---

take the initiative to seek a new minister. The "state of education" was a type of catechumenate where an individual's faith could be watched, observed, and encouraged until he/she became a regenerate member.

14. Clark, *Antiquities, Historicals and Graduates of Northampton*, 21. Clark had another date for their marriage: March 18, 1674. He claimed that Esther was a widow for five years before their marriage. However, this seems highly unlikely in the face of other evidence, especially of the record of her role in Stoddard's conversion. Esther Warham Stoddard was highly esteemed in Clark's work. He traced her influence on Northampton through her relationships to the ministers of the church there: Eleazer Mather and Solomon Stoddard (husbands), Jonathan Edwards (grandson), Solomon Williams (great great grandson), Samuel P. Williams (great great great grandson), and William S. Leavitt (great great great great grandson). Clark estimated that if her influence were measured through the length of their respective ministries in addition to her years of widowhood, it would yield a connection to the church at Northampton of 170 years.

15. Miller, "Solomon Stoddard: 1643–1729," 278.

16. See Appendix Document 3: ordination recorded in records of the First Church Northampton, MA.

and he did not disappoint them. However, they could never have imagined that this young twenty-six-year-old Harvard graduate would lead them well beyond "half-way" in his nearly 59 years as their pastor, nor the influence and controversy this man would generate in New England and in the life and ministry of his celebrated grandson, Jonathan Edwards.

> Northampton's greatest claim to fame from the 1670s to the 1730s . . . was Solomon Stoddard's success as a preacher. Stoddard's church became renowned for periodic revivals of piety, and his ecclesiology articulated the third phase of the Puritan experiment in New England communities. It appeared to Stoddard and many of his contemporaries that the children of the intensely religious founders were faltering in spiritual intensity. The third generation of religious leaders, coming to power in the 1670s and 1680s, labored inexhaustibly to recall their flocks to anxiety about eternal salvation. They revived the Calvinist program of discounting even highly moral "good works" and trusted only in Christ as the purchaser of God's saving grace for humankind. Impassioned denunciations of the sins of complacency have been labeled "jeremiads" by historians, a favorite sermon technique that linked the contemporary crises of the New England colonies . . . with the abandonment of their forefathers' spiritual mission. Stoddard excelled at the jeremiad, but he also provided a remarkably popular alternative vision of individual and communal spiritual commitment. He preached God's love as well as God's wrath, and he exhorted all who found in their hearts any ground of hope for salvation to come into the church. This was a shocking breach with the rules of earlier generations, for it dismissed not only testimony of experienced grace as the criterion for full church membership, but also the second generation's compromise of an additional "half-way" membership status for those who consented to be governed by Christian rules but lacked the "born-again" experience. After years of argument, Stoddard persuaded his church to open the Lord's Supper to all who were not openly sinful in life and to embrace that sacrament as a possible means of receiving God's saving grace.[17]

The controversy that swirled around Stoddard concerned his unique view of the Lord's Supper as a converting ordinance. Going beyond the Half-Way Covenant, he opened Communion to all who professed faith in Jesus Christ and whose lives were upright and free from

17. Tracy, "Solomon Stoddard," para. 3.

scandal. Stoddard believed that the Lord's Supper was a means of grace. Therefore, he allowed professing Christians, albeit unregenerate, to the Table which would expose them to that grace and might bring about their conversion.[18]

Was this an innovation or did he borrow the concept from elsewhere? Was this just a power-move trying to draw authority away from democratic Congregationalism to a more clergy-centered Presbyterian system? Why would Stoddard and Edwards, both of whom had such elevated views of God's glory and such passion for revival, come down on opposite sides of this issue? What motivated a solidly evangelical Stoddard to move even further beyond the liberalizing position of the Half-Way Covenant?

Other questions should be asked as well. How wide was Stoddard's influence on the churches of Massachusetts and Connecticut? Why did Increase Mather believe that Stoddardism would threaten to disrupt the order of religion and society by erasing the very distinction between the church as a sanctified body of believers and the secular community? What caused Stoddard to move from the position of an open Communion to one that viewed Communion as a converting ordinance? Did Stoddard actually believe that the Lord's Supper converted the unregenerate so that it could be given indiscriminately? Ralph Coffman suggests that Stoddard first passed through a Sacramental stage followed by an Evangelical stage where he experienced an awakened Christology and where Jesus Christ became more central in his preaching.[19] Is that an accurate inference based upon the data?

The background for this reflective and descriptive dissertation was formed by answering these questions in order to gain a clear and accurate definition of Stoddard's view of the Lord's Supper amidst the criticisms of opponents like Increase Mather, Edward Taylor, and even Jonathan Edwards himself. The author's personal interest in Stoddard stems from a twenty-five-year pastorate in Northampton, just two blocks away from

18. "In Stoddard's view, man was, of course, powerless to effect his own salvation, for that was the province of the Almighty. Stoddard emphasized instead the process whereby grace was conveyed from God to man through the ordinances of the Instituted Church. They were Christ's legacy and, as a consequence, the real historical significance of primitive Christianity. Christ died to redeem mankind and provided the means of redemption in the ordinances of baptism, prayer, scripture, preaching, censure, and the Lord's Supper." Lucas, "An Appeal to the Learned," 262.

19. Coffman, 157.

the Bridge Street Cemetery where Solomon, Esther, and son John have table-graves erected in their memory.

*Beyond the Half-Way Covenant: Solomon Stoddard's Understanding of the Lord's Supper as a Converting Ordinance* will seek to demonstrate three things: First, Stoddard's views can only be understood within the wider context of the decline of Puritanism and the liberalizing force of the Half-Way Covenant. Second, Stoddard's view of Communion grew out of his own study of English Puritanism and Scottish Presbyterianism, as well as his own conversion experience at the Lord's Table, and far from being a corrupting influence on the church in Northampton, became the very context for evangelical revival leading to five separate "harvests" in his nearly sixty years of ministry. Third, while Stoddard's view of Communion had an immediate impact on the Northampton church and the future ministry of Jonathan Edwards, it also had a wider influence on a significant number of churches in the Connecticut Valley.

The first chapter will examine the distinctiveness of English Puritanism in both its Separatist and non-Separatist forms. The chapter will trace the merger of these two forms into New England Congregationalism and the influence of John Cotton in establishing the experience of the new birth as the basis for church membership and town citizenship.

The second chapter will examine strict Congregationalism and will lead to a discussion of the Cambridge Platform of 1648 and the first colony-wide attempt to establish uniformity on polity, and the qualifications and procedures for church membership. Special attention will be given to the question of infant baptism and the need for a colony-wide policy that would eventually lead to the Synod of 1662, and the generational issues that brought about this liberalizing movement.

The third chapter will explore the historical context of the Connecticut Colony in relationship to the settling of Northampton, especially in connection to the demise and then startling resuscitation of the Half-Way Covenant among Connecticut churches. The chapter will also touch upon the growing alliance between church and town against the clergy and how this was exemplified by the unfortunate case of the strict Congregationalist Eleazer Mather. A look at the beginning of Solomon Stoddard's ministry will offer insight into his transition of 1677 and the beginning of his articulation of the Lord's Supper as a converting ordinance.

The fourth chapter will demonstrate how the development of Stoddard's view moved beyond the Half-Way Covenant and showed its relationship to the wider discussion of the Lord's Supper within English Puritanism, which formed a backdrop to Stoddard's thought. The chapter will also explore how his perspective won the day at the Reforming Synod of 1679, though not all of New England, and how he dealt with his critics.

The fifth chapter will assess Stoddardism according to the breadth of its influence in Western Massachusetts and the Connecticut Valley. The chapter will also discuss the influence of Stoddard's views on the ministry of his famous grandson, Jonathan Edwards, and how it led to the latter's dismissal from the Northampton church.[20]

A final afterword will present the "heart" of Stoddardism, which was the preaching of the "gospel" and the "conversion of sinners."

---

20. See Appendix Document 6: this was the only mention of Edwards' dismissal recorded in the original books of the First Church Northampton, Forbes Library, Northampton, MA.

# 1

## What Did It Mean to Be a Puritan?

> No one can really appreciate the ethos of Anglicanism without
> a recognition of how much it derives from nature, nor the char-
> acter of Puritanism apart from a realization of its dependence
> upon divine grace and revelation.[1]

WHILE ANGLICANS MAY DEBATE the accuracy of this quote, those whose
heritage flows back to English Calvinism would never for a moment
doubt its truth. John F. H. New contends that the Anglican system was
based upon "the unimpaired power of human reason,"[2] which is so evident in the works of Richard Hooker (1554–1600) as well as in Anglican
discipline and church order.

On the other hand, the Puritans believed that human reason
untouched by grace and unenlightened by revelation was a manifesta-
tion of fallen human nature. Thus the mind had to be shaped by the
Reformation principle *sola scriptura,* and from this fountainhead flowed
the Puritan understanding of life, as well as church order and discipline.
"The Puritans were above all else the people of the Book and what united
all Puritans was their belief in the Bible as the sole authority."[3]

The Puritans wanted to reform the Anglican Church based upon
the New Testament pattern of the primitive church and mediated by
what they considered the classic Protestant position, which differed
among the various groups of Puritans. The Elizabethan Settlement
(1558–1603)[4] disappointed those who were committed to the principles

1. Cook, "The Church," 15.

2. New, *Anglican and Puritan,* 6.

3. Elton, *England under the Tudors,* 425.

4. Protestantism flourished under Edward VI, was truncated and persecuted under
Catholic Mary Tudor, and was once again established under Elizabeth I. She declared

1

of the Reformation. They "could not content themselves with a reformation that reformed so little. Elizabeth to their dismay did not reform the church but only swept the rubbish behind the door."[5]

The Thomas Cartwright lectures of 1570 argued that implementing this pattern of reform could only be accomplished by abolishing ecclesiastical hierarchy and replacing it with a system of discipline (akin to Presbyterianism modeled after Calvin in Geneva) designed to bring the visible church more in line with the invisible church as a gathering of "visible saints." Although Cartwright's views[6] got him expelled from his professorship at Cambridge, and in spite of Edmund Morgan's critique that the first Reformers "were blind to the sin of their own complacency,"[7] this concept that the visible church must accurately reflect the Christian character and profession of its members became the driving force behind Puritan ecclesiology.

Striving for the Puritan ideal took place both within and outside the Church of England. From the 1570s to the middle of the 1590s there was an extensive Puritan movement within the church, and men such as John Field and Thomas Wilcox led a Presbyterian-like system complete with synods and assemblies—all within the established church. These assemblies met for fellowship and preaching that encouraged a more purified form of the Christian faith—a church within the church.[8] While this movement declined with Field's death in 1588, the Puritan movement within the church continued beyond the death of Elizabeth and on into the reigns of James I (1603–1625) and Charles I (1625–1649) and the days of the Long Parliament.

---

independence of the Church of England from Rome in the Act of Supremacy of 1559. However, her version of Protestantism differed from that of Edward VI. She struck a "middle way" between Protestantism and Catholicism.

5. Haller, *The Rise of Puritanism*, 8.

6. Cartwright's views were that each parish should elect their own elders and ministers; the national church should be formed by representative synods; there should be an equality of all government in church and state.

7. Morgan, *The History of a Puritan Idea*, 2.

8. A very interesting point is made by Francis Bremer in his paper on "Congregations before Congregationalism," para. 10. His comments help explain further the concept of fellowship that took place within the Puritan congregations, and also how "Presbyterianism" came to mean something different in New England than it did during the Elizabethan Settlement.

An excerpt from Larzer Ziff illustrates how some Puritan congregations actually existed within an Anglican structure. John Cotton formed a congregation of the "redeemed" within his Anglican parish church in England. In 1617, the Bishop (who had suspended and then reinstated Cotton for his Puritan practices) appointed Edward Wright as the chaplain of the parish in order to preside over the elements of the service containing ceremonies to which the Puritans objected. The following is the description of what must have occurred in the church each Sunday. Ziff writes: "An interesting shuffle took place on a Sunday on the steps of St. Botolph's as the Puritan members waited until the Apostle's Creed, at which their orthodox fellow members would stand, was completed under the direction of Chaplain Wright and then filed in to hear Cotton's sermon while the Anglicans passed on their way out."[9]

It was during the decade of the 1630s that the Great Puritan Migration to America took place. These nonconforming but nonseparating Puritans founded the Massachusetts Bay Colony at Salem, and subsequent migrations established settlements in Dorchester, Watertown, Charlestown, Roxbury, and Saugus as well as a central settlement in Boston.

Alongside this Puritan (and more Presbyterian) movement within the Church of England, there developed a separatist movement of Puritans who were also Calvinistic, but who did not believe that the established church was the true church. The leaders of this movement were such men as Robert Browne (1550?–1633) and Robert Harrison (154?–1585?). Browne became the more radical dissident in his separatist views, even attacking the writings of Thomas Cartwright. Browne's major tracts were *A Book Which Sheweth the Life and Manners of All True Christians* (1582); *A Treatise upon 23 of Matthewe*; and *Treatise of Reformation without Tarrying for Anie* (1582, published in Holland). Browne has been an easy target for criticism due to his numerous inconsistencies: for being too radical in his separatist views; for flirting with Anabaptism; and for reconciling with the Church of England to regain some of his personal freedoms as well as employment. However, all of this did not hinder his influence or the spread of his views on Congregationalism and theology. His writings were major contributions in the early development of religious dissent and were the beginnings of the English Separatist movement during the later reign of Elizabeth

9. Ziff, *The Career of John Cotton*, 50–51.

I. "The term Brownists was a common designation for early Separatists before 1620. Brownists, Independents, and Separatists were all used somewhat interchangeably for those nonconformists who broke with the Church of England."[10]

These Separatists held to a Congregational polity which rejected any idea of a national church, although associations of churches were acceptable to them. They believed that the church was a people called out of the world by the Gospel, bound together in a voluntary covenant, with membership composed of those who professed faith in Jesus Christ and desired to live a life worthy of Him.

> The Separatists kept alive the Puritan idea of the church in those years following the demise of the Presbyterian movement in the 1590s. And their stand quickened the consciences of the non-separating Puritans as they implemented in practice what Puritan doctrine demanded in theory. The movement grew, attracting men of considerable ability such as Henry Ainsworth and John Robinson, whose congregation finally settled at Leyden in Holland in 1609 and later provided the Pilgrim Fathers who in 1620 founded the first permanent settlement in New England at New Plymouth.[11]

Once in New England, the Puritans, both non-Separatists and the Pilgrim Separatists, became inextricably connected. Larzer Ziff claims that when John Endicot, leader of the settlement at Salem, "brooded about the practical details of just how such a reformed body could be gathered—he consulted the avowed Separatists at Plymouth and copied their procedure on every essential."[12]

On the other hand, historical evidence also exists that demonstrates the influence was greater in the other direction.[13] In either case, both Puritan movements recognized that separation from the Church of England had occurred and that even the "Great Migration" of the non-Separatists had also become a great separation. Both Pilgrims and Puritans established churches that were ordered according to the

---

10. "English Dissenters: Brownists," para. 1.

11. Cook, 22.

12. Ziff, *Puritanism in America*, 50.

13. Cook, 28.

Congregational pattern owing to the writings of William Ames,[14] Robert Parker, and others.

There was, however, one distinction between Puritans and Pilgrims, which should not be overlooked. This distinction had to do with the requirements for church membership. It was the practice of the Pilgrim Separatists to allow professing Christians of upright moral character to enter their membership without testifying to any experience of regenerating grace. However, the non-separating Puritans required as a condition of membership that a person not only owned the covenant of grace through a profession of faith in Jesus Christ, but could also give testimony to the experience of saving grace. This underscored the distinction made by Augustine and Calvin between covenant grace (visible church) and saving grace (invisible church).

It was John Cotton more than anyone else in Puritan New England who made the examination of one's regenerative experience a prerequisite for church membership. "By 1635, however, with John Cotton probably leading the way, the leaders of the Bay Colony reached this significant corporate decision. They made a narration of the experience of regenerating grace a requirement of adult church membership. Seen in full perspective, this was a radical demand. For the first time in Christendom, a state church with vigorous conceptions of enforced uniformity in belief and practice was requiring an internal, experimental test of church membership."[15]

Puritans had always been concerned with trying to explain conversion and the work of God in the human soul. In fact, Francis Bremer states that conversion was at the very heart of the Puritan movement.[16] Puritans were predominately Calvinists and every Calvinist believed that salvation was not the result of human action, but the work of God in the hearts of those whom God predestined in Christ. As the Westminster Confession of Faith (1646) framed it: "Those of mankind that are predestinated unto life, God, before the foundation of the world was laid, according to His eternal and immutable purpose, and the secret counsel

---

14. It was Congregationalist William Ames and his authoritative summary of theology, i.e., *The Marrow of Sacred Divinity*, to whom the New England Puritans would especially defer because in his writings they found the very foundation of many of their doctrines. Vaughan, *The Puritan Tradition in America*, 35.

15. Ahlstrom, 148.

16. Bremer, para. 3.

and good pleasure of His will, has chosen, in Christ, unto everlasting glory, out of His mere free grace and love, without any foresight of faith, or good works, or perseverance in either of them, or any other thing in the creature, as conditions, or causes moving Him thereunto; and all to the praise of His glorious grace."[17]

It was one thing to work this doctrine out within the context of the Church of England. It was quite another thing to work it out in the social context of a New World. And the issue that seemed to refract the once clear unified beam of predestination was the concept of "preparation." If conversion was completely a work of God's electing grace, what then was the responsibility of the sinner who had no ability to save himself? Furthermore, if salvation was sovereignly distributed only to the elect, what were the moral and spiritual responsibilities of a person who had not yet confirmed his election through regeneration and faith?

This was of utmost importance as the New England experiment would face spiritual decline if people refused obedience to the "external covenant," i.e., the ordering of one's life according to the doctrine and morality of the Christian Faith. As Perry Miller asks, "With what right, then, could divines press upon ordinary men the obligations of the external covenant? Were they not impotent?"[18] Yes, they were impotent to save themselves, says Miller, but not impotent to prepare themselves for salvation and to fulfill the moral obligations of the national covenant.

> They found at once that the conception [of preparation] had so-
> cial bearings. A man undergoing a work of preparation, in the
> hope it may be followed by the successive works [of regenera-
> tion, etc.], will endeavor to perfect his external behavior. He may
> finally go to hell, but if in this world he lives by endeavor, he
> automatically fulfills the national terms. As Puritans perforce
> became more concerned with power than purity, they labored
> to make the moral incentive of the national covenant do what
> the founders had gratuitously assumed would be done by regula-
> tions, fines, and the stocks.[19]

Miller overstates his argument and continues to show his consistent criticism of the hypocrisy of Puritanism. He also draws an unfortunate conclusion that Hooker and Shepherd cracked open the door to

17. *Westminster Confession of Faith*, Chapter III; Article V.
18. Miller, *Mind*, 54.
19. Ibid., 56.

Arminianism for future generations because of their emphasis on human ability in their preparationist theology.[20] Such a charge can only come from one who does not understand the nuances. No Puritan would ever countenance salvation through a gradual improvement of the human condition. As Thomas Schafer remarks, "The differences between saving grace and common grace don't lie in the degree, but in the nature of them."[21]

Calvin taught that man is morally depraved and can do nothing in his own welfare in regard to salvation. Solomon Stoddard himself sounded very much like Calvin when he graphically stated: "That original sin that reigns in every natural man is the fountain of every abomination. Every natural man is over-run with the leprosy of sin from head to foot; has not one spark of goodness in him; all his faculties are corrupted utterly. His whole Soul is like a dead carcass, like a heap of carrion, lothsome and noisome, and God may justly abhor him; which evidently shews a great necessity for his conversion."[22]

Thus, Stoddard and his Puritan heritage uniformly agreed that human ability had no place in conversion. However, most would also have agreed that a person must be "prepared" before faith and conversion took place, and that somehow such preparation was a part of man's natural state. In fact, in the preface of *Guide to Christ*, Stoddard mentioned such men as Perkins, Sibbes, Preston, Hooker, Shepherd, and Norton as all supporting the necessity of preparation.

At the very foundation of Stoddard's doctrine of conversion was the understanding that the unregenerate sinner can do something to prepare for conversion. He along with Thomas Hooker believed that there were two steps of preparation: conviction and humiliation. "There are two degrees of this preparation: the first is Awakening, whereby the sinner is convinced of a present necessity of peace and reconciliation with God; whereby he is put upon a diligent use of all means in order to obtain his salvation: the other is Humiliation, whereby the sinner is brought out of himself, and off from his carnal confidences, to yield himself a Prisoner to God: until the soul be humbled as he is not capable of faith."[23]

20. White, "Were Hooker and Shepherd Closet Arminians?" 35.

21. Schafer, "Solomon Stoddard and the Theology of Revival," 335.

22. Solomon Stoddard, *A Treatise Concerning Conversion [1719]*, 95–96. (Republished as *The Nature of Saving Conversion*.)

23. Stoddard, *The Safety of Appearing*, 205.

John Cotton was distinct in that he did not hold a well-formed doctrine of preparation. He believed that a man was as passive in his second
birth as he was in his first. However, Cotton's denial of preparation may
not be as "cut and dried" as Miller implies. David Parnham claims that
all Puritans, including John Cotton, were practitioners of preparation
and that each had his own preparationist theology.

> Even the less law-minded of Puritans could esteem the con-
> science-shaking gift of preparation. This, as Mark Dever has
> noted in a study of Richard Sibbes, could be thought of as a gift
> of the Holy Spirit. And no less a "spiritist" than John Cotton
> acknowledged that the Spirit works preparatively upon the un-
> converted, first by binding them "under the sense of [divine]
> wrath unto fear of Damnation" and then—having come as an
> "earthquake" to press them "down to the nethermost hell"—by
> requiring them to experience a "burning" and "blasting" of the
> "iron" heart's "fleshly" piety, a renunciation of "false confidence"
> in "legal" deeds. But Cotton, insistent advocate of free grace, was
> not one to distend the preparatory process.[24]

Thus Ann Hutchinson believed that John Cotton and her brother-
in-law John Wheelwright were the only Puritans who truly preached the
doctrine of grace. She and her husband had sat under Cotton's teaching
in England and followed him when he came to Boston. As Miller says,
"She wrapped herself in the mantle of John Cotton, protesting that she
had merely repeated his sermons."[25] She held to a free grace denial of the
work of preparation and that sanctification was not evidence of justification. She also believed that the Holy Spirit dwelled in the justified, and
came close to implying personal and immediate revelation apart from
the Bible.[26] Her views challenged the Puritan understanding that salvation was completely a work of grace and that moral conduct was not
a necessary authentication of God's grace. Thus she was charged with
"antinomianism," i.e., without law, and banished with her followers to
Rhode Island.

After Hutchinson's banishment by the General Court in 1637,
John Cotton defended himself on sixteen points before a three-week
synod overseen by Thomas Hooker and Peter Bulkeley in Newtown,

---

24. Parnham, "Redeeming Free Grace," 917.

25. Miller, *Mind*, 59.

26. Morgan, *The Puritan Dilemma*, 124.

Massachusetts, in August of that same year. It is not clear whether Cotton completely satisfied his questioners. He was trying to defend himself and Ann Hutchinson, while at the same time trying to distinguish himself from her. Some historians claim that the arguments on both sides were so nuanced that they were saying the same thing but using hair-splitting language. Ultimately, it was John Winthrop who protected Cotton[27] and it was Cotton's grandson Cotton Mather, who in his *Magnalia Christi Americana* preserved his grandfather's legacy by distracting his readers from seeing any central responsibility borne by John Cotton in the controversy.

> But the warm sunshine will produce a swarm of insects; whilst matters were going on thus prosperously, the cunning and malice of Satan, to break the prosperity of the churches, brought in a generation of hypocrites, who "crept in unawares, turning the grace of our God into lasciviousness." A company of Antinomian and Familistical[28] sectaries were strangely crouded in among our more orthodox planters; by the artifices of which busie opinionists there was a dangerous blow given, first unto faith, and so unto the peace of the churches. In the storm thus raised, it is incredible what obloquy came to cast upon Mr. Cotton, as if he had been the patron of these destroyers; merely because they, willing to have a "great person in admiration, because of advantage," falsely used the name of this "great person," by the credit thereof to disseminate and dissemble their errors. . . . 'Tis true, such was Mr. Cotton's holy ingenuity, that when he perceived the advantage which erroneous and heretical persons in his church had from his abused charity taken to spread their dangerous opinions, before he was aware of them, he did publickly sometimes with tears bewail it, "that the enemy had sown so many tares whilst he had been asleep."[29]

The Cambridge Platform of 1648 tightened the bolts on the New England Way, which had been shaken to the core by such dissension and controversy. The independence of the churches in the Massachusetts

27. Miller, *Mind*, 61.

28. "Familism" was a catch-all term used especially by Hooker in the free grace controversy in New England. Familism was named after the late-sixteenth-century "Family of Love," founded by the Dutch mystic Hendrik Niclaes. It was a particular strand of Antinomianism that included such heretical doctrines as mortalism, deification, perfectibility, and revelations of the Spirit that were honored above Scripture.

29. Cotton Mather, *Magnalia*, 71–72.

Bay Colony provided no ecclesiastical mechanism to cope with the far-reaching issues of this grand experiment: issues like the aforementioned antinomianism controversy, and the crisis surrounding Roger Williams. There was also the issue of those who were perceived as a presbyterial threat to New England Congregationalism, like Benjamin Hull of the Weymouth Church, as well as his replacement Robert Lenthall.[30]

In all of these situations, the clergy clearly needed to appeal to the civil magistrate and the General Court for rulings and punishment. At the same time, there was a real fear that the government was gaining too much power and tipping the scales on the balance of power. This was especially apparent when the Massachusetts General Court tried to limit the number of weekday lectures held in the colony.

There were also a number of unresolved ecclesiastical matters surrounding the issues of baptism of children and of church membership for recent immigrants from England.

> The number of these baptized non-members was increasing, and they were joined in their dissatisfaction by many new migrants who had been church members in England but found on arriving in Massachusetts Bay that their children were ineligible for baptism because the migrants themselves, despite their membership in churches in the homeland, were judged unfit for admission to the colony's churches. These groups, then, with their dissatisfaction over eligibility requirements for baptism and membership, were naturally brought into alliance with colonists who favored presbyterial style polity. The Scottish form of church government not only provided for synods with power to compel conformity, it also admitted most parish residents to the churches and administered the first sacrament to their children. Thus, if all complaining factions combined forces and obtained support from England, it was conceivable that Massachusetts Bay might be forced to adopt a church polity similar in many respects to that in Scotland.[31]

Several ministers petitioned the General Court to convene a meeting of churches in order to create an agreement or platform on church organization. They were motivated by the recognition that "differences of opinion and practice of one church from another do already appear amongst us & others (if not timely prevented) are speedily to ensue, &

30. Burg, "The Cambridge Platform," 476.
31. Ibid., 478.

this not only in lesser things."[32] The first session of the synod began to meet in September 1646 and lasted two weeks.

The second session was interrupted in June 1647 by an epidemic, which took the lives of the venerable Thomas Hooker and the wife of Governor John Winthrop. The third and final session in August 1648 brought about an important document on Congregational polity with Richard Mather as its chief architect. Henry Wilder Foote mentions that the synod kept no records apart from its final document.[33] This document represented a deliberate rejection of the English Presbyterian polity that had recently been set forth in the Westminster Assembly's "Westminster Confession of Faith" (1648) and "Form of Presbyterial Church Government" (1645). The full title was *The Cambridge Platform: A Platform of Church Discipline Gathered out of the Word of God; and Agreed upon by the Elders and Messengers of the Churches Assembled in the Synod at Cambridge in New England to be Presented to the Churches and General Court for their Consideration and Acceptance in the Lord.*

While the Platform is considered to be "one of the greatest creations of the founding fathers, and it remained the standard symbol of Congregationalism in Massachusetts throughout the colonial period and in Connecticut until the Saybrook Platform of 1708,"[34] there were portions of it that would have to be reconfigured for a new generation. The portion most vulnerable to change was Chapter XII having to do with the admission of members into the church:

1. The doors of the churches of Christ upon earth do not by God's appointment stand so wide open, that all sorts of people, good or bad, may freely enter therein at their pleasure; but such as are admitted thereto, as members, ought to be examined and tried first, whether they be fit and meet to be received into church society or not.

2. The things which are requisite to be found in all church members are repentance from sin, and faith in Jesus Christ; and therefore these are the things whereof men are to be examined at their admission into the church, and which then they must profess and hold forth in such sort as may satisfy "rational charity."

32. Vaughan, 98.

33. Foote, "The Significance of the Cambridge Platform of 1648," 29.

34. Smith et al., *American Christianity*, 129.

3. The weakest measure of faith is to be accepted in those that desire to be admitted into the church, because weak Christians, if sincere, have the substance of that faith, repentance and holiness, which is required in church members; and such have most need of the ordinances for their confirmation and growth in grace.

4. In case any, through excessive fear or other infirmity, be unable to make their personal relation of their spiritual estate in public, it is sufficient that the elders, having received private satisfaction, make relation thereof in public before the church, they testifying their assents thereunto; this being the way that tends most to edification.

5. A personal and public confession and declaring of God's manner of working upon the soul, is both lawful, expedient, and useful in sundry respects and upon sundry grounds.

6. This profession of faith and repentance, as it must be made by such at their admission that were never in church-society before; so nothing hinders but the same way also be performed by such as have formerly been members of some other church, and the church to which they now join themselves as members may lawfully require the same.

7. The like trial is to be required from such members of the church as were born in the same, or received their membership, or were baptized in their infancy or minority by virtue of the covenant of their parents, when being grown up unto years of discretion, they shall desire to be made partakers of the Lord's Supper; unto which, because holy things must not be given unto the unworthy, therefore it is requisite that these, as well as others, should come to their trial and examination, and manifest their faith and repentance by an open profession thereof, before they are received to the Lord's Supper, and otherwise not to be admitted thereunto.[35]

The Platform affirmed a strict requirement for church membership espoused by John Cotton in his treatise *Of the Holiness of Church Members*, where he raised the bar by saying that it was "the duty of all the members of the particular visible church to be truly regenerate." [36] There had to be a public "relation" or testimony of conversion. In the case of

35. *The Cambridge Platform*, XII: 1–7.
36. Miller, *Orthodoxy in Massachusetts*, 196.

those who were too fearful to do so, they could make their "relation" to the elders who would make it public on their behalf. However, in spite of the acknowledgment that hypocrites were capable of feigning their testimony and slipping into membership, the act of examination was still essential for determining the constituents of the visible church. "The important thing, they were bound to admit, was the profession; they knew it was desirable for examiners to test the sincerity of the profession, but the externality of the act was after all its essential part."[37]

On the other hand, the Platform did not address the questions that were particularly pressing to the second generation of Puritans. What was to be done with the children of morally upright but not yet converted parents? What was to be done with these unconverted parents, who were themselves baptized as infants? While they were to be put "under church watch," what was their status since they were not in full communion and could not take the Lord's Supper? These questions produced a variety of practices throughout the Colony as Puritanism morphed. A decade and a half later, the answer would come in the form of the Half-Way Covenant. That answer, however, would take Puritanism in an unforeseen direction and Solomon Stoddard would take it further still.

37. Ibid., 198.

# 2

## The Half-Way Covenant

> The doors of Christ's churches on earth do not stand so wide open that all sorts of people, good or bad, may freely enter as they desire. Those who are admitted to church membership must first be examined and tested as to whether they are ready to be received into church fellowship or not. . . . These things are required of all church members: repentance from sin and faith in Jesus Christ. Therefore repentance and faith are the things about which individuals must be examined before they are granted membership in a church, and they must profess and demonstrate these in such a way as to satisfy rational charity that they are genuinely present.[1]

THUS THE CAMBRIDGE PLATFORM marked the height of American Puritanism's attempt to create a church where visible membership closely approximated the invisible. The Platform defined a Congregational church as "part of the militant visible church . . . a company of saints by calling, united in one holy body, by one holy covenant, for the public worship of God, and the mutual edification of one another in the fellowship of the Lord Jesus."[2] Both Augustine and Calvin acknowledged the difference between covenant grace (visible church) and saving grace (invisible church), and the inability of any one person to determine the elect. Yet New England Puritanism, though it viewed the covenant as mutual and voluntary, still insisted that the covenanters must be by "charitable discretion . . . accounted Saints by calling."[3] "The stones that were to be laid in Solomon's Temple were squared and made ready be-

---

1. *The Cambridge Platform*, XII: 2.
2. Ibid., II: 6.
3. Ibid., III: 2.

fore they were laid in the building. . . . And, wherefore so, if not to hold forth that no members were to be received into the church of Christ, but such as were rough-hewn, and squared, and fitted to lie close and level to Christ and to his members."[4]

The Cambridge Platform had little impact upon the reform movement that was taking place at the same time in England, culminating in the Puritan Commonwealth and Protectorate under Cromwell (1649–1660). The "Middle Way" of New England Congregationalism was in no way attractive to English Presbyterians who, while in agreement with the concept of a national church, disagreed with the Platform's Congregational polity. Nor did the Platform appeal to English Independents who, while agreeing with the principles of Congregationalism, disagreed with the Platform's lack of toleration for any religious group that was not Congregational.[5]

There was also sharp criticism leveled against the Platform by European Puritans at the notion of a regenerative membership. Dutch minister William Apollonius asked whether it was true that no one would be admitted into the visible church "unless he is endowed with the real internal holiness of regeneration and with justifying faith in Christ. Must such a person undergo a strict examination?"[6] Was there not the danger of misreading the heart of a person and leaving out of visible membership a true saint? What if the "relation" or testimony of an elect person did not convince the minister or congregation of his election? The New England Puritan would admit that while hypocrites slipped through the cracks, it was still better to err on the side of leaving out a true saint than to knowingly include a hypocritical sinner.

Sir Richard Saltonstall, who was a former resident of New England, wrote John Cotton in 1650 from England of his concern regarding the rigidity of American Puritanism: "It doth not a little grieve my spirit to hear what sad things are reported daily of your tyranny and persecutions in New England, as you fine, whip, and imprison men for their consciences. . . . Truly, friends, this your practice of compelling any in matters of worship to do that whereof they are not fully persuaded is to

---

4. Fleming, *Children and Puritanism*, 39.

5. Stout, *The New England Soul*, 52–53.

6. Tipson, "The Judgment of Charity," 460.

make them sin . . . and many are made hypocrites thereby, conforming their outward man for fear of punishment."[7]

And in reply, John Cotton said, "If it did so, yet better to be hypocrites than prophane persons. Hypocrites give God part of his due, the outward man, but the prophane person giveth God neither the outward or inward man."[8]

American Puritanism's attempt at creating a pure church also created a number of issues which were to haunt its future. First, as already discussed, the emphasis on visible saints separated New England from Old England (both Reformed and Anglican) and its exclusionary practices made the New England Puritan churches become "Out-cast" and "Sion"[9] to those in Europe. Second, New England Puritans, by their emphasis on a regenerative membership, separated themselves from the world and lost perspective on their evangelical function. Third, New England Puritans, by their emphasis on an examined church membership, separated themselves from the next generation.

It is this last point that is crucial in understanding the Half-Way Covenant. If it was true that New England was the New Israel, as John Norton had portrayed it, then it was also true that it would be the second generation of Puritans who would enter the Promised Land. And, continuing the analogy, if the Cambridge Platform was the "Law of Moses," then what did the "Law" have to say about the children of the second generation?

> By saints, we understand: Such as have not only attained the knowledge of the principles of religion, and are free from gross and open scandals, but also do, together with the profession of their faith and repentance, walk in blameless obedience to the Word, so as that in charitable discretion they may be accounted saints by calling (though perhaps some or more of them be unsound and hypocrites inwardly) because the members of such particular churches are commonly by the Holy Ghost called "saints and faithful brethren in Christ"; and sundry churches have been reproved for receiving, and suffering such persons to continue in fellowship among them, as have been offensive and

7. Hutchinson, *Collection of Papers*, 203.

8. Ibid., 132.

9. Terms used by John Norton in 1661 in an election sermon. "Out-cast" referred to the New England Way's rejection by Anglican Restoration England under Charles II. "Sion" is a Hebrew word which means barren, forsaken, and undesirable.

scandalous; the name of God also, by this means, is blasphemed, and the holy things of God defiled and profaned, the hearts of the godly grieved, and the wicked themselves hardened and helped forward to damnation. The example of such does endanger the sanctity of others; a little leaven leavens the whole lump.

The like trial is to be required from such members of the church as were born in the same, or received their membership, or were baptized in their infancy or minority by virtue of the covenant of their parents, when being grown up unto years of discretion, they shall desire to be made partakers of the Lord's Supper; unto which, because holy things must not be given unto the unworthy, therefore it is requisite that these, as well as others, should come to their trial and examination, and manifest their faith and repentance by an open profession thereof, before they are received to the Lord's Supper, and otherwise not to be admitted thereunto. Yet these church members that were so born, or received in their childhood, before they are capable of being made partakers of full communion, have many privileges which others (not church members) have not: they are in covenant with God, have the seal thereof upon them, viz: baptism; and so, if not regenerated, yet are in a more hopeful way of attaining regenerating grace, and all the spiritual blessings, both of the covenant and seal; they are also under church watch, and consequently subject to the reprehensions, admonitions and censures thereof, for their healing and amendment, as need shall require.[10]

Perry Miller claims that the Cambridge Platform "shamefully hedged"[11] on the issue of infant baptism, barely addressed the status of the children who were not able to profess faith in Christ, and said nothing at all about their children. It was already acknowledged by most churches that only the children of regenerate members were entitled to baptism, and that these children entered a kind of religious apprenticeship until as adults they could affirm their baptism by relating an experience of conversion and therefore enter into full membership. It was not enough that these second generation adults could claim a work of grace nurtured by baptism and a godly home, or even testify of a personal response to the Gospel, as the Anabaptists would frame it. These adults had to give a "relation" or testimony of saving grace that conformed to a very definitive process of conversion. According to Robert Pope, "the

10. *The Cambridge Platform*, III:2; XII:7.
11. Miller, *Mind*, 90.

*morphology of conversion*, initially developed by the English Puritan divines as a guide for individual souls, was transformed into a yardstick for measuring the faithful."[12] The Platform did not address the situation incurred if these second generation adults never satisfied the test for "relation," nor did it offer guidance on whether they would be entitled to baptize their children or grandchildren.[13]

Puritanism was generally clear on its view of the Lord's Supper because it concerned adults and not children. It was not a means of grace, but a seal of grace—a confirmation of the covenant set forth in the Gospel. And in New England, Communion was given only to those adults in full membership—those who could recount their conversion to the satisfaction of the church. It should be noted, however, that there were earlier examples in New England of the practice of "open Communion,"[14] which was evidence that this position was held by post-Reformation Protestants other than Solomon Stoddard.[15]

In contrast, Puritanism was not as clear on the subject of baptism because it concerned children and not adults. Puritanism in both its Congregational and Presbyterian forms historically practiced infant baptism, showing their direct descendency from John Calvin.

> If reason is listened to, it will undoubtedly appear that baptism is properly administered to infants as a thing due to them. The Lord did not anciently bestow circumcision upon them without making them partakers of all the things signified by circumcision. He would have deluded his people with mere imposture, had he quieted them with fallacious symbols: the very idea is shocking. In the Old Testament the Lord distinctly declares, that

12. Pope, *The Halfway Covenant*, 5.

13. Cooper, *Tenacious of Their Liberties*, 89. Cooper states that John Cotton, as early as 1634, supported the position that a grandchild could be baptized on the strength of his grandfather's full church membership, although Cotton did reverse his position after a few years.

14. Pope, 255–256.

15. "His [Stoddard's] notion that the Lord's Supper was a 'converting ordinance' originated in a rudimentary form during a sixteenth-century debate among Reformed theologians in Germany and Switzerland. The doctrine was further developed by the English Erastian, William Prynne, and subsequently refined by John Humfrey (1621–1710), the non-conformist vicar of Frome Selwood in Somersetshire. Humfrey directly influenced Stoddard and numerous other theologians. The Stoddardean controversy was part of a wider English discussion that had its roots in earlier continental debates." Holifield, "The Intellectual Sources for Stoddardism," 374.

the circumcision of the infant will be instead a seal of the promise of the covenant. But if the covenant remains firm and fixed, it is no less applicable to the children of Christians in the present day, than to the children of the Jews under the Old Testament. Now, if they are partakers of the thing signified, how can they be denied the sign? If they obtain the reality, how can they be refused the figure? . . . The objection, that there was a fixed day for circumcision, is a mere quibble. We admit that we are not now, like the Jews, tied down to certain days; but when the Lord declares that though he prescribes no day, yet he is pleased that infants shall be formally admitted to his covenant, what more do we ask?[16]

Anabaptists (in any era) would find Calvin's arguments unconvincing and based on reason and inference rather than Scripture. However, New England Puritans would not allow any such anti-paedobaptist idea to flourish and therefore grounded their view of infant baptism firmly on the concept of the Federal Covenant and as a parallel to Old Testament circumcision (Gen 17).[17] The Puritans believed there was only one covenant of grace in both dispensations of the Old and New Testaments. Consequently, they also believed in only one Gospel in both dispensations, which proclaimed a salvation through the Promised Lord, Jesus Christ. This Gospel was preached to Abraham, who believed God and was justified by faith (Gal 3:6–8). However, this Covenant of Grace was made not only to Abraham but also to his seed (Gal 3:16). And just as circumcision[18] was the sign and seal of Abraham's righteousness of faith (Rom 4:11), so baptism is the sign and seal of the covenant of grace in any age. It was Richard Mather who said, "We do not believe that Baptisme doth make men Members of the Church, nor that it is to be administered to them that are without the Church, as the way and means

---

16. Calvin, *Institutes of the Christian Religion*, 4:16.5.

17. The problem with too close a relationship between circumcision and baptism is that it tends to equalize the internal reality of faith with external ritual. This was shown by the opponents to the Synod of 1662, such as Chauncy and Davenport, who had to redraw some lines of distinction between the Old Testament church and the New Testament church.

18. "To equate the circumcision of the old covenant with the baptism of the new covenant evidently does two things: it exalts circumcision to a height of significance it never had in Israel . . . and it diminishes the uniqueness and power of the New Testament rite that is rooted in the cross and resurrection of Jesus Christ." Beasley-Murray, *Baptism in the New Testament*, 341.

to bring them in, but to them that are within the Church, as a seale to confirme the covenant of God unto them."[19]

However, in spite of all the theoretical emphasis on the covenant of grace and its inclusion of the children of the saints, it accomplished very little in practice. John Cotton had to admit that the children of believers were not holy with regenerating grace, "but only with that holiness whereby they are admitted to the means of grace, with promise of efficacy to the elect seed, and offers thereof to the rest, as far as to leave them without excuse."[20]

A few years later Increase Mather would say that covenant children could be sure that God's "line of election" ran "through the loins of [their] Parents." However, he would also add that this line could never be taken for granted because converting grace "is of absolute necessity in the order of Salvation, and that as to the Children of godly Parents as well as others."[21] Thus in a very real sense, the Puritans' understanding of baptism was severely limited both by their understanding of election and by their fear that the sacrament would be regarded as a means of grace.

The real hope of the first generation of Puritans was that their baptized children would be nurtured within the preaching and discipline of the church, and that these children would grow to adulthood and would confirm their place in the covenant of grace by their own experience of grace. Thus they would become full members of the covenant community and carry on the same hope to their children. However, this hope was not forthcoming and triggered a controversy first appearing in the 1640s, which lasted all the way through to the Great Awakening.

> Then, in addition to the two great divisions of the early days—the consciously regenerate and those who laid no claim to Christian character—there arose a third class of the population . . . a class of men and women whose parents had been actively Christian, who had themselves been baptized and educated in the Christian faith, were well grounded in the knowledge of Christian truth, were students of the Bible and interested listeners in the sanctuary, who were desirous of bringing up their families in a way in which they themselves had been trained, and who were moral and earnest in their lives; yet could lay no claim to such an experience as that which their parents had called a change of heart,

19. Miller, *Mind*, 87.

20. De Jong, *The Covenant Idea*, 89.

21. Stout, 96.

and when asked as to any conscious work of God in their souls were compelled to admit that they could speak with confidence of none.[22]

This controversy was not due to the failure of the Gospel, but to the insatiable desire of the New England Puritan for purity, and what seems like the presumptuous peeking into men's souls. David Boorman engages in an "if only" scenario by wondering how different things might have been "had the tests for membership and access to the Lord's Supper been different . . . had a profession of faith and a moral life remained the criteria of membership . . . had more confidence been placed in the promise of the covenant of grace."[23] Solomon Stoddard would have agreed with this assessment, but his perspective awaits our fuller examination.

There were a number of options that the churches in New England could have pursued in order to deal with the decline in church membership of the second generation. A first option would have been to go back to the original position of the Pilgrims (and other Reformed paedobaptist groups) and offer membership and the Lord's Supper to all who made a profession of faith and whose lives were morally upright. The second option would have been to continue to deny any church privilege or standing to the baptized yet unregenerate adult children of full members. The third option was to extend baptism to the children of those who had been baptized but remained unregenerate.

This last option had been debated for years before the Synod of 1662. It was supported chiefly by Richard Mather, who in 1645 had proposed extending baptism to all the children of church members and had prepared such a recommendation to be included in the Cambridge Platform.[24] It was not included, however, because it was a "lightning rod" issue and would have caused open division. John Cotton was also in favor of "extended baptism" and claimed that though these infants "be not fit to make such a profession of visible faith, as to admit them to the Lord's Table, yet they may make such a profession full enough (through their parents who were full members) to receive them to baptism."[25]

However, extended baptism was opposed by the likes of Thomas Hooker, Charles Chauncy, Increase Mather and John Davenport. The

22. Walker, *The Creeds and Platforms of Congregationalism*, 263–264.

23. Boorman, "The Half-Way Covenant," 83.

24. Ibid., 87.

25. De Jong, 101.

Massachusetts General Court as early as 1646 recognized the existence of these differing views and feared the repercussions of disunity among and within the churches. Therefore, just as it called for the Cambridge Synod, the Court called for a ministerial assembly in 1657 to discuss this issue.

The gathered clergy produced a document written chiefly by Richard Mather which was titled *A Disputation Concerning Church Members and Their Children in Answer to XXI Questions*. This document was the "official" position of the New England Puritans as well as the basis for what would come to be known as the Half-Way Covenant of 1662.[26] Richard Mather argued that adults who were baptized as children were "external" or "outward" members of the church who could have their children baptized if they "understand the grounds of Religion, are not scandalous, and solemnly own the Covenant in their own persons, wherein they give up both themselves and their children unto the Lord and desire Baptism for them."[27]

Those in agreement with this position did not believe it was a compromise to the covenant of grace since everyone already recognized that these children were not "saved" by their baptism. Once again, a reference was made to Old Testament Israel by the recognition that not all who were a part of the external covenant were members of true Israel. And since not all of New England's "external members" were saved, these unregenerate were denied full church membership, which included the Lord Supper as well as the vote.

Though this position may have become "official" due to the Synod of 1657, it did not bring unity among the churches and succeeded in creating rifts between ministers and their congregations. For example, Richard Mather was unable to convince his own Dorchester church to follow his lead on extended baptism and ultimately backed down for the sake of unity. "Churches debated, procrastinated, defied their ministers, or bowed to clerical pressure, but without resolving the problem. Order and unity disappeared and each day things became more unsettled. To compound the difficulty, the restoration of Charles II in 1660 in England

---

26. "The term 'Halfway Covenant' probably originated in the 1760s when the followers of Jonathan Edwards renewed the debate over the extension of baptism to the children of non-regenerate parents. I have found the term used for the first time in Joseph Bellamy's *The Halfway Covenant: A Dialogue*, New Haven, 1769. The term never appeared in the controversy which followed the so-called Halfway Synod." Pope, 8.

27. Stout, 59.

jeopardized the Puritan cause everywhere. Now more than ever New England had to close ranks."[28]

Once again the General Court intervened and called for a synod so that an official decision could be reached and the issue finally laid to rest. In March 1662, more than seventy clergy and lay delegates gathered at the First Church in Boston and debated the seven propositions written by Richard Mather five years earlier. The same deep rift existed, but this time those in favor of extended baptism won the day by a seven to one margin.

*The Answer of the Elders and Other Messengers of the Churches, Assembled at Boston in the Year 1662* addressed the question, "Who are the subjects of baptism?" Most important of the seven propositions were:

Proposition 2: The Members of the Visible Church according to the Scripture, are Confederate Visible Believers in particular Churches, and their Infant Seed, i.e., Children in Minority, whose next Parents, one or both, are in Covenant.

Proposition 3: The Infant-Seed of Confederate Visible Believers, are Members of the same Church with their Parents, and when grown up, are personally under the Watch, Discipline, and Government of that Church.

Proposition 4: These adult Persons, are not therefore to be admitted to full Communion, merely because they are and continue Members, without such further Qualifications, as the Word of God requireth thereunto.

Proposition 5: Church-Members who were admitted in the minority, understanding the Doctrine of Faith, and publickly professing their assent thereunto; not scandalous in Life, and solemnly owning the Covenant[29] before the Church, wherein they give up

---

28. Pope, 41–42.

29. "I do heartily take and avouch this one God who is made known to us in the Scripture by the name of God the Father, and God the Son even Jesus Christ, and God the Holy Ghost to be my God, according to the tenor of the Covenant of Grace; Wherein he hath promised to be a God to the Faithful and their seed after them in their Generations, and taketh them to be his People, and therefore unfeignedly repenting of all my sins, I do give up myself wholly unto this God to believe in, love, serve and Obey Him sincerely and faithfully according to this written word, against all the temptations of the Devil, the World, and my own flesh and this unto death. I do also consent to be a Member of this particular Church, promising to continue steadfastly in fellowship with it, in the public Worship of God, to submit to the Order, Discipline and Government

themselves and their children to the Lord, and subject themselves to the Government of Christ in the Church, their Children are to be baptized.[30]

Almost immediately the presses in Cambridge were turning out a publication: *Anti-Synodalia Scripta Americana* by Charles Chauncy. The dissenters called the decision an "innovation." They were afraid that allowing the unregenerate even into external membership would pollute the church and defile the Lord's Supper. Also, they believed that those who did not fulfill their baptismal vows were covenant breakers and should not be allowed to baptize their children.

The majority decision of the Synod did not settle very much because within a congregational system every local church made up its own mind on the issues. Thus the "Half-Way Covenant," a result of the Synod of 1662, did not gain approval by most churches for decades.[31] Nevertheless it did become the "official" position of New England Puritanism and there was one thing that was settled: "both the idea and the ideal of a pure church were virtually sacrificed in 1662."[32]

The Puritans on both sides of the extended baptism issue could be perceived as guilty of pragmatism. Those in favor were motivated by a very practical concern that the second generation and beyond would be lost to a declining church if something were not done to keep them in the covenant. Those against extended baptism were also motivated by a fear of church decline if the purity of a regenerate membership were not maintained. The debate could be summarized as the pragmatism of progeny versus the pragmatism of purity; both sides were able to marshal scriptural support for their positions, an art form which the Puritans had mastered. Also, both sides were in agreement that baptism and the Lord's Supper differed in their nature. Baptism was a seal of covenant holiness, while the Lord's Supper was a sacrament of spiri-

---

of Christ in it, and the Ministerial teaching, guidance and oversight of the Elders of it, and to the brotherly watch of Fellow Members: and all this according to God's Word, and by the grace of our Lord Jesus enabling me thereunto. Amen." Ross, "The Half-Way Covenant," para. 11.

30. Smith, 203–4.

31. Pope argues that, in most cases, the lay members were not willing to immediately accept the terms of the Synod. Most were divided over the subject of extended baptism for a long time and when they did finally accept it, if at all, the covenant was adapted to fit their own situation.

32. Boorman, 97.

tual growth.[33] The latter demanded the ability to examine oneself and to discern the Lord's Body, which was only within the capability of the regenerate membership.

In hindsight, however, the conclusion of the Synod of 1662 was the only real option available that would preserve the Puritan ideal of "a moral, covenanted society (including every citizen) and truly reformed churches (made up only of the elect.)"[34] By allowing the baptized children of full members into the external covenant, the Puritans hoped to maintain a godly society. By allowing only the regenerate into full membership with the privilege of the Lord's Supper, the Puritans hoped to maintain a godly and pure church.

It would be Solomon Stoddard who would soon come to center stage by going even beyond the Half-Way Covenant. He would suggest that a proper understanding of the external, national covenant would require that all citizens should be allowed to take the Lord's Supper, which was not a seal of regeneration, but of Christ's willingness to covenant Himself with the nation.[35] In doing so, Stoddard would pry apart the Puritan integration between society and church, which had tried to preserve the idea of a pure church while striving to manage a moral society at the same time. Instead, Stoddard would open up the church to become an outpost for the Gospel in society. Perry Miller calls Stoddard "the first great revivalist in New England" who "inaugurated the era of revivalism on the American frontier."[36]

33. Ibid., 93.
34. Noll, *America's God*, 40.
35. Stoddard, *Inexcusableness*, 12, 20.
36. Miller, "Solomon Stoddard," 316, 319.

# 3

## Northampton and the Half-Way Covenant

[The Half-Way Covenant] doth tend in the end of the worke (how good soever the end of the worke was) to shake & undermine the fundamentall doctrine & practice of the Congregationall way, viz., that visible Saints are only matter [and qualified for full communion]. . . . It now stands them in hand, who were of the Synod of 62, to looke to the maintaining of the defence which they p[re]pared . . . fore the securing of the churches: from pollution by unpr[e]pared ones incroaching upon full communion in the Lord's Supper and voting.[1]

So wrote John Russell, minister of the church at Hadley, Massachusetts, to Increase Mather while the latter was still an opponent of the Half-Way Covenant. Russell's concern was that the same liberalizing force which was at work in the Synod of 1662 would continue its influence by allowing the unconverted into full membership, thus polluting the Lord's Supper.

Just across the Connecticut River to the west from Hadley was Northampton, where, in May 1653, twenty-four people petitioned the General Court for permission to "plant, possess and inhabit Nonotuck."[2] The land was purchased from the Nonotuck[3] tribe in September 1653, and some of the original landowners were John Pynchon and Elizur Holyoke. The men were cousins, prominent citizens of Springfield, Massachusetts, just south of Northampton, and came from a tradition of Connecticut Presbyterianism.[4] The land was then settled in 1654 largely

---

1. Russell, "Collections," 83–84.
2. "Historic Highlights," para. 1.
3. Nonotuck means "midst of the river."
4. Trumbull, 6–12.

by former Connecticut residents.[5] They bore the influence of Thomas Hooker and John Warham who had founded the Connecticut Colony because they disagreed with the connection between regenerate church membership and civil enfranchisement, i.e., the right to vote, made by churches of the Massachusetts Bay Colony. Thus the churches along the Connecticut River Valley early on evidenced a moderate form of Puritanism.

Northampton built its first meeting house in 1655 and Eleazer Mather came to candidate as the town's first pastor in late 1658. A church was formally gathered there in 1661 and Joseph Eliot of Roxbury was called to be Mather's assistant. The records do not indicate a reason, but Eliot did not last a full two years.[6] Mather's difficult ministry lasted until his untimely death in 1669 at the age of thirty-two. The fact that a church was gathered after a meeting house was built indicates that the town was originated as a civil body where every man had equal influence and position. This was in distinction to earlier settlements where the church was established first as the basis for social and political hierarchy. Thus in Northampton the town meeting remained open to all, which was the early influence of settlers coming from congregations in Connecticut where church and town meeting were almost identical. Before 1661, the town of Northampton would hold weekly services led by various lay-men, but official worship services would not be held nor the sacrament celebrated until a minister was selected.

The town of Northampton continued to grow more rapidly than its church. By 1660 the population was probably between three and four hundred. By 1669 ninety-eight men were on the land rolls indicating a population exceeding five hundred.

> Of these, seventy persons entered Mather's church as members in full standing and were admitted to the Lord's Supper. . . . Of forty-eight male settlers between 1653 and 1658, twenty-three were admitted to Communion. Of seventeen newcomers in 1659

---

5. Sweeney, "River Gods and Related Minor Deities," 68. Sweeney acknowledges that "a majority of settlers who established the towns of Northampton, Hadley, and Hatfield in the 1650s and 1660s had come from the Connecticut towns of Windsor, Hartford, and Wethersfield."

6. Clark, *Historical Catalogue*, 2–3. Also, see this dissertation's Appendix Document 1 for a copy of the original entry in the Northampton Church Records of its "gathering"; and Document 8 for a list of signatures to the original church covenant, including Eleazar and Esther Mather—from the Forbes Library in Northampton, MA.

and 1660, only seven came to full communion status. And of thirty-three between 1661 and 1669, only six had been admitted when Mather died. There were, however, 162 other persons who had entered into some relationship with the church either through baptism or through association with their parents.... At any rate, Mather's [regenerate] membership was somewhat less than half his congregation, and his visible saints numbered about one-third of the [total] adults of his congregation and the town.[7]

Eleazer Mather, unlike his father Richard who essentially drafted the propositions of the Synod of 1662, was strongly opposed to the new measures and essentially blocked many people in the church and the town who wished to adopt the Half-Way Covenant. During this period, however, there were many more settlers who came to Northampton from the churches of Hartford, Wethersfield, and Windsor, thus increasing the numbers of those who favored the half-way measures.

The dissension and factionalism among the churches of the Connecticut Colony almost made Massachusetts Congregationalism look unified. There was the evangelical Congregationalism of Thomas Hooker of Hartford; the moderate Congregationalism of Samuel Stone of Hartford; the rigid Congregationalism of Henry Whitefield of New Haven and Richard Blynman of New London; and the "erratic" Congregationalism of John Warham of Windsor. There was also the Presbyterianism of Gershom Bulkeley of New London, John Haynes of Hartford and John Woodbridge Jr. of Killingsworth.[8]

The Connecticut General Court called for a Synod in 1667 to settle the anticlerical dissensions and fragmentation plaguing the churches. The attempt was doomed from the very start when the rigid Congregationalists objected to the term "synod."[9] The only substantial detail to emerge from this gathering was a recommendation that the Connecticut Assembly pass a law of toleration for all "approved ac-

---

7. Behnke, "Solomon Stoddard of Northampton," 29.

8. Paul Lucas indicates that most of these Presbyterians graduated from Harvard College, which in the 1650s and 1660s was a place of religious and political turmoil. He stops short of saying that it was the seed-bed of Presbyterianism, but acknowledges that class of '64 graduate Solomon Stoddard's personal library was absent "some of the standard works of English and New England Congregationalism, while conspicuous was *The Due Right of Presbyteries* and several other volumes by the Scottish Presbyterian Samuel Rutherford." Lucas, *Valley*, 60.

9. Ibid., 67.

cording to lawe, orthodox and sound in the fundamentals of Christian religion."[10] In Connecticut, this toleration was directed primarily towards Presbyterians.

Amidst and because of all this dissension, something unexpected occurred; the Half-Way Covenant experienced a stunning resuscitation after being pronounced all but dead in the Connecticut Colony. The Covenant, which had previously languished because it had neither the support of the clergy nor the laity, received surprising support from an unlikely source: the "unchurched" members of the town.

> Showing little interest in the theological questions swirling around extended baptism or satellite membership, the unchurched used the covenant as a lever to expand their challenge to the autonomy of exclusiveness, and authority of the church. Consequently the more a minister or a majority of members, or both, belittled the covenant, the more the nonmembers demanded the town meeting impose it. The attitudes of the unchurched provided considerable impetus for the 1667 Synod to find a solution for the turmoil resulting from towns trying to exercise ecclesiastical authority.[11]

An example of this was a situation in the First Church of Windsor, Connecticut, where its aged minister, John Warham (the father of Esther Warham Mather Stoddard), decided to abandon the Half-Way Covenant in 1664. However, when it was made known in 1667 that Warham was sick and wanted to step down as minister, the town of Windsor pressed to have a vote in the selection of his replacement. The General Assembly of Connecticut allowed the issue to be settled by a vote of the town, and Nathaniel Chauncey was chosen over Henry Wolcott to be the new minister. Chauncey was selected because he was pro-covenant and that is exactly what the town wanted. Therefore, the Windsor Church once again became a Half-Way Covenant church.[12]

Another reason for the resuscitation of the Half-Way Covenant in the Connecticut Colony was the acute awareness of the failure of the churches to bring any kind of moral or spiritual influence on society. The years of acrimonious disagreements between the churches, and between clergy and laity of those churches, had drained energy and attention

10. Felt, *The Ecclesiastical History of New England,* 468.

11. Lucas, *Valley,* 74.

12. Ibid., 79.

away from their primary calling. Instead of creating a pure church and a transformed society, churches were failing on both counts. For example, records of the Windsor, Connecticut, church show that it added only 1.5 new members per year between 1639 and 1677, a figure that represented negative growth when deaths and withdrawals were taken into consideration.[13]

In response to this failure, some churches in the Connecticut River Valley, like Northampton, created a type of lay reformation that strived to overcome the languid state of Puritan Congregationalism. Congregationalism had historically relied upon the power of the church covenant. This idea was at the very center of Thomas Hooker's understanding of the Congregational system in order to provide moral and unifying power.[14] However, these individual church covenants driven by the authority of the clergy had failed to provide either morality or unity, and so something else was needed. This lay reformation found its motivational source not in ministerial authority, but in the initiative taken by the "fraternity" of the church to end factionalism and institute new standards of moral behavior for churched and non-churched alike. At the heart of this reformation of morals was the adoption and adaptation of the Half-Way Covenant to fit the needs of each church.

Many historians disagree as to the significance of the Half-Way Covenant. Some see it as a part of the decline of Puritan spirituality, while other historians see it as the result of changing demographics and the natural adaptation of the Puritan idea of church membership for a new generation. However, James Cooper clearly sums up both the need for and impact of the Half-Way Covenant, and although he speaks primarily of churches in Massachusetts, what he says was appropriate to Connecticut churches as well:

> The Half-Way Covenant generated a crisis . . . that surpassed all others in the seventeenth century in its breadth and lasting consequences. For the first time in the Bay's brief history, the Massachusetts clergy were significantly and publicly divided over vital issues of church order. The loss of unanimity permanently eroded clerical authority in church affairs, forcing a more active role in government upon ordinary churchgoers.

13. *Records of the First Congregational Church of Windsor, Connecticut,* Vol. 1: membership lists.

14. Hooker, *A Survey of the Summe of Church-Discipline,* 46–50.

The controversy also undermined the intellectual foundations of Congregationalism. Facing two openly conflicting interpretations of biblical warrant, many lay people could no longer understand Congregationalism as merely a set of procedures and principles that flowed inevitably from Scripture. The struggle over the Half-Way Covenant, in sum, set into motion currents that would continue to reshape Congregationalism and lay–clerical relations for the rest of the colonial era.[15]

Although there are no church records that indicate an anti-Mather or church vs. town controversy over the Half-Way Covenant in Northampton, there is evidence that there was controversy, which may have contributed to Mather's poor health and his assistant's (Joseph Eliot) hasty departure.[16] Since Mather was incapacitated by his illness in 1667, he could not provide leadership to the anti-Covenant faction within the church. Therefore, those that favored the new measures gained a majority and ultimately won the day, being supported by the town. The records of the Northampton First Church call the victory "this day of our reformation" and contains an extensive document several times the length of the original church covenant. This document was written and given to the minister on his death bed, and can be condensed as follows:

> Disclaiming all Confidence of, or any worthinesse in ourselves to be in Covenant with God [we] . . . promise and Covenant to keep and seek the commandments of God, and to walk in obedience, learning, and doing whatsoever the Lord hath, or hereafter shall reveale and make known to us his mind and will. . . . We further promise and engage tearfully and conscientiously to avoid all strife, contention, evil surmising, perverse disputings, whisperings, envy, schisms, pernicious opinions contrary to sound doctrine, and whatsoever all may find to weaken union . . . disturb peace, interrupt communion, together with all the causes and occasions of them, but constantly . . . to seek after things that make for peace, and the things wherewith we may edify one another, ministering to one another . . . by frequent exhortations, constant watchfulness and seasonable admonition . . . till we grow up into a perfect majesty in Christ's name. These things we all promise as before the Lord. . . . We are humbly bold to insist that . . . miscarriages and comings short, contrary to the settlements and resolutions of our hearts, shall not make void this Covenant. . . . Now, because of all this we make a covenant in the behalft of

15. Cooper, 89.
16. Lucas, *Valley*, 84.

ourselves and our little ones, confirmed and assent to this day, and unfayntedly engage ourselves, and our hearts, and subscribe our names thereunto.[17]

After the church had written this new covenant, it proceeded to approve the Half-Way Covenant in November 1668,[18] and extended baptism to the children of baptized non-members by placing the latter under "church watch." However, the church adapted the Half-Way Covenant even beyond the intent of the Synod of 1662. In the church records there was a new section entitled *Propositions concluded by the church at Northampton this 29th of the 10th month and the 12th of the 11th month (1668). [Regarding] Duty and Privilege of the Children of the Covenant and the due and ordinary management thereof.*[19] Under this section were listed seven propositions. Proposition five declared that all baptized persons became members in "a state of education" and were marked for full membership when "they shall be judged upon due examination to hold forth such an experimental work of faith." This unique state of education was no doubt in deference to Mather's supporters who wanted to protect some semblance of a regenerate membership and most likely the reason why the Half-Way Covenant passed unanimously by congregational vote.

However, the church did not stop its adaptation process at this point. On November 5, 1672, just one month after Solomon Stoddard was ordained, the church went one step further and basically eliminated the "state of education" by allowing all baptized persons who were morally upright and owned, i.e., agreed to, the covenant of the church to become full members when they reached adulthood. "That from year to year such as grow up to adult age in the church shall present themselves to the elders, so if they be found to understand and assent to the Doctrine of faith, not to be scandalous in life, to be willing to subject themselves to the government of Christ and this church, shall publickly

---

17. *Records of the Northampton First Church,* Vol. 1.

18. The identities of the signers of the original covenant are found in the *Northampton Church Records* (18–4–1661), and Trumbull, 86–117. Their places of origin and date of arrival in Northampton can be calculated using the *Judd Manuscripts,* 121, 173, 183–187, 504. The *Northampton Town Records* indicate that Mather was granted land by a town vote on January 4, 1659, and that home lots for Mather's "Dorchester friends" were granted on November 25, 1659.

19. *Records of the Northampton First Church,* Vol. 1.

own the covenant to be acknowledged members of this church. Neh. 10:28, 29; Isa. 44:5."[20]

This additional step of 1672 clearly shows that the church had already begun to move away from the narrative of one's conversion experience as the basis of full membership. "In Northampton, as in many towns, the narrative simply became excess baggage."[21] While most churches adopted the Half-Way Covenant by 1690, not all were as liberal as Northampton in their adaptation. And while the new measures helped to reduce tensions between church and town, the conflict between the laity and clergy increased as the sad story of Eleazer Mather's death-bed conflict with his church exemplifies.

Eleazer Mather died on July 24, 1669, and was buried in the Bridge Street cemetery, a small white limestone spire marking his grave. His widow was left with a young daughter and two sons, and an estate of 524 pounds, of which 60 pounds were in books. Church records do not indicate when Solomon Stoddard started to preach at Northampton, although Ralph Coffman claims that he accepted a three-month trial and started his regular preaching duties on March 4, 1670.[22]

It is also known that on August 29, 1670, a committee of nine men was appointed by the town (not the church) to follow through on a settlement agreement first arranged when Stoddard was offered the job.[23] The records show a sense of hesitation by Stoddard throughout the process, as if he was "dragging his feet" for some reason. Although he continued to preach, he did not formally accept the settlement agreement until February 7, 1672, and was not ordained until September 11th of that same year.

The reason for such hesitation may have been due to his lack of certainty as to his own spiritual condition. Stoddard had been baptized in the Boston church of his father Anthony Stoddard. However, because he was never able to give testimony as to his conversion, Solomon Stoddard had never entered into full membership nor had he ever received the Lord's Supper.

---

20. Ibid. See Appendix Document 2 for original entry from *Northampton First Church Records*; thanks to the Forbes Library in Northampton, MA.

21. Lucas, *Valley*, 137. Lucas also says that this 1672 reform made possible the eventual elimination of the conversion narrative in 1714.

22. Coffman, 59.

23. Coney, "Jonathan Edwards and the Northampton Church Controversy," 42.

While Lucas claims that this decision to go to Northampton reflected Stoddard's unpredictability and thirst to be different,[24] could it rather have reflected his own lack of religious certainty? Also, the fact that he chose Northampton may have indicated that he felt a kinship with the more latitudinarian religious developments in Connecticut than he did with the Massachusetts Bay Colony and Boston.

Some of the oral traditions about Stoddard's early years in Northampton, mentioned in the Judd Manuscripts,[25] were based upon the reporting of a Pastor Lathrop of West Springfield. He claimed that Esther Mather Stoddard was convinced that her husband was unconverted and therefore started regular weekly prayer meetings among the ladies of the town praying for his conversion. Whether there is any truth to this remains debatable, but someone's prayers were answered sometime before April 1672, because Solomon Stoddard had a conversion experience while he was celebrating Communion.

> One Sabbath as he was at the table administering the Lord's Supper, he had a new and wonderful revelation of the Gospel scheme. He caught such a full and glorious view of Christ and his great love for men as shown in his redemptive work, that he was almost overpowered with emotion, and with difficulty went forward with the communion service. By reason of this peculiar experience of his he was led to think, that the place where the soul was likely to receive spiritual light and understanding was at the Lord's Table—that there, in a special manner, Christ would present to reveal himself, in all his fullness of love to the souls of men.[26]

Stoddard became a full member of the church on April 4, 1672, and submitted to ordination on September 11, 1672.[27] Thus he was in full compliance with the pure church concept of early Puritanism as codified by the Cambridge Platform. Church records show that at the beginning of Stoddard's ministry, 133 people entered into various forms of church membership ranging from full membership to those who entered with their parents, those baptized as infants, those who personally agreed to the covenant, and those who entered into the "state of education." In fact,

24. Lucas, *Valley*, 146.

25. W. Stoddard, "Solomon Stoddard," 42.

26. Tarbox, "Jonathan Edwards as a Man," 625–626.

27. See original dated entry of Stoddard's ordination from the *Northampton First Church Records* in Appendix; thanks to the Forbes Library in Northampton, Massachusetts.

on November 5, 1672, Stoddard made an entry into the church records stating "a form of the words expressing the summe of the Covenant to be used in the admission of [young] members into the State of Education":

> _____ [name] you do here publickly take hold of the covenant of the Lord as a grace bestowing covenant subjecting yourself to the teachings and government of Jesus Christ in his church and engage according to your place and power to promote the welfare of it: and we do here publickly acknowledge you as a member of the church of Christ in a state of education, promising to watch over you for the good of your soule, to take care of your instruction and government in the Lord, and to make you partaker of all such privileges as by the rules of Christ belong to you.[28]

A look at the Northampton church record book indicates that Stoddard kept very close documentation of all new members, carefully delineating the particular form of membership for each. As has already been mentioned, in 1672 there were 133 people listed as entering some state of membership in the church. The majority of these either owned the covenant (forty-five) or entered the church through being baptized (eighty-two). The records show at least twelve different categories of membership ranging from personally owning the covenant to being admitted as full members.

However, in 1677, without any prior indications, Stoddard ceased keeping track of these various forms of membership.[29] Coffman may be overstating the case when he uses the term "revolutionary" to describe this action, but he is accurate in pointing out that what Stoddard did was very significant.

> Then, on November 5, 1677, silently and without warning, the first revolution in American history began. On that day Stoddard simply stopped recording whether his parishioners were either full members or Half-Way members of the church in Northampton. The brashness of the action was matched by the modesty of the revolutionary—the Northampton Minister had just introduced the beginnings of modern democracy into America by cutting the Gordian knot of Massachusetts' charter

28. *Northampton First Church Records*, November 5, 1672. See original entry in Appendix Document 4 from the Forbes Library in Northampton, MA. Note the one-line reference to Jonathan Edwards' ordination dated 22 February, 1726/7.

29. Walsh, "Solomon Stoddard's Open Communion," 110.

that limited citizenship to those who were judged truly regenerate Christians by their pastors.[30]

He began the practice of receiving into full membership all who
were morally upright and who professed faith in Christ. Once they were
members, they could have their children baptized and had the right and
responsibility of receiving the Lord's Supper.

> Then, in 1677, without warning, without so much as a by-your-
> leave, least of all from Increase Mather, he [Stoddard] closed
> the separate account of baptisms. Thereafter— secure in his
> Congregational autonomy but still more in his frontier remote-
> ness— he baptized every adult who assented to the articles of
> faith, and admitted him to the Supper. He treated the congrega-
> tion and virtually the whole town (there were still a few resolute
> sinners) as the church; at one stroke he cut his way through the
> maze of the covenants by identifying the church not with the
> society of saints but with the town meeting.[31]

Stoddard came to the realization that the Half-Way Covenant did
not work and, at the same time, it worked too well. It was his observation that these half-way measures allowed for a kind of indifference
on the part of those who would become half-way members. They could
remain half-way committed, thus escaping further responsibility to
nurture their own souls and come under the scrutiny of the church as
full members, as well as escaping certain responsibilities of citizenship.[32]
However, even more disconcerting to Stoddard was that these half-way
measures also seemed to produce an extreme conscientiousness on
the part of some about the Lord's Supper; some were afraid to become
full members and have to approach the Table lest they might accrue to
themselves judgment.

> The fearful introspection of the New England communicant
> emerged clearly in Samuel Sewall's diary. Sewall joined the
> church in 1677 with hope that God would "communicate him-
> self" in the sacrament, but he was "afraid that because I came to
> the ordinance without belief, that for the abuse of Christ, I might

---

30. Coffman, 43.

31. Miller, *Mind*, 227

32. "But shortly after 1665 an awful result became evident: because citizenship
meant obligation, masses of good people found themselves content to stop with the
half-way position in order to evade it." Ibid., 127.

be stricken dead." Sewall considered fleeing from the meeting-house. But he feared that such a course would leave him unfit for the next sacrament, and he "thought it would be strange for me who was just then joined to the church to withdraw, wherefore I stayed." Even then, Sewall could "hardly sit down to the Lord's Table," so terror-stricken was he. The entire experience was painful; after Sewall convinced himself to receive the sacrament, his hopes that Christ would proffer "some glimpse of himself" were disappointed, and although he was not "stricken dead," he did not record his first communion with any sense of joy.[33]

Ministers who ferociously disagreed on the nature and use of the Lord's Supper were in agreement about their parishioners' fears about approaching the Lord's Table. Stoddard decried this and preached on how many people neglected Communion from a "meekness of conscience, fearing they have liberty to come."[34] Edward Taylor of Westfield, a strict Congregationalist who opposed the Half-Way Covenant and did not agree with Stoddard concerning much else, also lamented this condition. "What a lamentation is this! Persons professing the gospel, religious in their lives, knowing in the concerns of religion and the things of God, orderly walkers in their conversation, attending God's worship public in assemblies, private in their families, secret in their closets, and filled with experiences of God treating of them in His Word, yet miserably neglecting this wedden supper. Oh! What a lamentation! Certainly they fall under rebuke from our doctrine for their neglect."[35]

Just as strict Puritanism ultimately produced confusion about the sacrament of Baptism, so the Synod of 1662 ultimately produced confusion about the sacrament of Communion. Although ministers agreed that there was a problem, they did not readily agree on the solution.[36] One thing was for certain, however: there was a definitive shift in emphasis on teaching the importance of and defining the duties of bap-

33. Holifield, "The Renaissance of Sacramental Piety," 42–43.

34. Stoddard, *Three Sermons Lately Preached*, 108. Also see Stoddard, *Inexcusableness*, 25.

35. Taylor, *Treatise Concerning the Lord's Supper*, 24–25.

36. Stoddard's father-in-law, the revered John Warham, spent much of his later life (died in 1670) struggling with his own sense of unworthiness to take Communion. William Stoddard records that Warham would often refuse to take the elements for himself when he administered the Lord's Supper to his congregation. Perhaps Esther herself struggled with this as well, which may have made this situation profoundly personal for Solomon. (W. Stoddard, *A Liberal*, 50.)

tized members in relation to the Lord's Supper. This was evidenced by a sharp increase in the printing of pamphlets on the importance of the Lord's Supper. Holifield claims that there were twenty-one editions of Communion manuals printed during the period of 1690–1738, compared to just eight manuals printed from 1739–1790.[37]

Cotton Mather decried the "Multitudes, and Quantities" of New Englanders who did "daily turn their Backs upon the Table of the Lord Jesus. . . . [When I see] whole Scores of People going away from the Table that has the Bread of Life upon it; then, The Fire Burns, my Heart is hot within me, and I cannot Suppress the just indication of my Sorrowes at so Unchristian a practice in those that will yet be called Christians."[38]

Ministers such as Mather warned the baptized of their duty to come to the Lord's Table and yet, at the same time, they still emphasized the necessity of saving grace being present in the communicant. This set up a dilemma for the over-scrupulous who lacked the assurance of their salvation. In an attempt to hold onto the New England Puritan tradition that grace was discernable, Cotton Mather relaxed his own requirement for the Lord's Supper by claiming that the visible saint need have no assurance of salvation.

At Second Church in Boston, Mather required of communicants only a profession of faith, showing their knowledge and belief, and a statement of "hope," oral or written, that the "Grace of God" had quickened their souls. While holding to the formal requirements established by the first generation, Mather tried to relax them just enough to attract potential communicants who feared the consequences of unworthy reception."[39]

Mather did not step out of tradition at this point as some in the first generation of New England Puritanism agreed that perfect assurance was not required of communicants.[40] "Those ministers, however, had not pleaded with the doubtful to advance a claim for the sacrament. Mather was pleading."[41]

37. Holifield, *Renaissance*, 48.

38. Mather, *A Companion for Communicants*, 62.

39. Holifield, *Renaissance*, 44.

40. Hooker, *A Preparative to the Lords Supper*, 350, 369–372; John Cotton, *The Way of the Churches of Christ*, 5, 73.

41. Holifield, *Renaissance*, 43.

In contrast, Solomon Stoddard disagreed that the solution was found in watering down the understanding of conversion by allowing those who were doubtful of their own salvation to proceed as if they were saved. This, he feared, would only blind them further to their own unregenerate condition.[42] Instead, he advocated the position that the Lord's Supper should be open to all who were moral and orthodox in their faith even if they were unregenerate so that they might expose themselves to the grace of God and be converted.

This then was the context of Solomon Stoddard's thought: his personal spiritual struggle with the certainty of his own salvation, his conversion at the Lord's Table and possibly an additional "conversion" later in his ministry;[43] the influences of English Puritanism on his view of the Lord's Supper, and his studies of the influential works of Scottish Presbyterians at Harvard. In addition, there was the impact of the Half-Way Covenant in the decline of sacramental piety, which, in turn, stimulated a renewed interest in New England to draw more over-scrupulous church members to the Lord's Table.

All of these were like seeds that, when planted into the receptive soil of Northampton, produced a harvest of evangelical influence which would have wide impact in the Connecticut Valley. Stoddard's influence, which would reach beyond his own generation, would move many churches beyond the Half-Way Covenant. However, this movement would also produce a new passion for the revival of religion and the winning of men's souls through the preaching of the Gospel.

42. "If these persons be told that this ordinance be only for Converted persons, yet if they after serious Examination have hope that they are converted, they may and ought to come; That will not satisfy their tender Consciences: they will say, We may have such hopes and yet not be Converted." Stoddard, *The Safety of Appearing*, 88.

43. Lucas, "Solomon Stoddard and the Origins of the Great Awakening," 748.

# 4

# Stoddardism[1]: Beyond the Half-Way Covenant

As the renown of those Reformers is a bulwark against those Errors that were Exploded by them, so we find ourselves embarrassed by their mistakes from proceeding in the work of Reformation: As if it were criminal not to mistake with them. . . . Men are wont to make a great noise that we are bringing in of Innovations, and depart from the Old Way: But it is beyond me to find out wherein the iniquity does lye. We may see cause to alter some practices of our Fathers, without despising of them, without priding ourselves in our own Wisdom, without Apostacy, without abusing the advantages that God has given us, without a spirit of compliance with corrupt men, without inclinations to Superstition, without making disturbances in the Church of God: And there is no reason that it should be turned as a reproach upon us. . . . Surely it is commendable for us to Examine the practises of our Fathers; we have no sufficient reason to take practises upon trust from them: let them have as high a character as belong to them, yet we may not look upon their principles as Oracles.[2]

THE NEW ENGLAND WAY was in deep trouble and Solomon Stoddard believed that the fault lay at the feet of the Founders.[3] They had been

1. I prefer the term "Stoddardism," which was used in the eighteenth century and is sometimes still used. However, another common term to describe the concept of open Communion today is "Stoddardeanism."

2. Stoddard, *Inexcusableness*, preface.

3. "The Puritan understanding of the special relationship between God and His people had changed. Stoddard tried to reflect and define that change. The Mathers denied it; they were defending the New England Way, a system of belief that was no longer viable. Solomon Stoddard was the vanguard of those who returned to scripture for guidance and found the old Puritan beliefs static and inflexible. New England had changed profoundly in the first one hundred years of its history. It is only reasonable to

too preoccupied with the precise nature of the elusive primitive New Testament church.[4] Yet their concern for discipline and polity had fomented a history of bickering and disunity. They had tried to create a pure church made up of the elect while at the same time creating a morally covenanted society.[5] However, this synthesis started to unravel in the second generation. Issues arose concerning the status of those baptized adults who did not have the experience of personal regeneration and whether or not they had the right to baptize their children.

Many believed that the Synod of 1662 would preserve this synthesis between theology and society by allowing those still unregenerate to participate in both church and social covenants. However, by withholding from them the Lord's Supper (the privilege of full membership), Puritans such as Increase and Cotton Mather believed they could maintain the centrality of a pure membership and the integrity of the New England Way.

Solomon Stoddard disagreed with them. He believed that the Half-Way Covenant did not go far enough, and what was needed was a reformation that separated "the integrity of the gospel and the divinely ordained prerogatives of a Christian nation."[6] Stoddard argued: first, that the Lord's Supper was not primarily a seal of personal regeneration, but a part of the worship of God which should be open to all who professed faith in Jesus Christ, whether or not they were regenerated;[7] second, that the Lord's Supper was open to all because God's relationship to New England was not based on a covenant with particular churches, but with the nation itself, or what he called "the Commonwealth of Israel."[8] Just as every Jew, saint or not, was required to be circumcised and to celebrate the Passover, so every Christian was to participate in the sacraments of Baptism and the Lord's Supper.[9]

---

expect that the common understanding of faith and practice would be altered as well. The Mathers, as guardians of the past, focused on Solomon Stoddard as the threat to their future." Jones, *Shattered Synthesis*, 61–62.

4. Lucas, *Valley*, 151.

5. Pope, 261.

6. Noll, 41.

7. Stoddard, *Inexcusableness*, 12, 20.

8. Solomon Stoddard, *Appeal to the Learned*, 69.

9. Walsh, 107.

It is not known when Stoddard started making his views on Communion public; however, we do know that his understanding of open Communion was not an innovation, but part of a wider discussion that had been going on in English Puritanism for three decades.[10]

> "Stoddardeanism" was no isolated event on the colonial frontier, and Stoddard himself was no innovator. He was the conscious heir of an identifiable sacramental tradition within the Reformed community. And though that tradition originated as a rationale for state control of the church, it eventually developed into a genuine expression of Reformed piety. It would be unfair to describe Humphrey or Timson, for example, as ecclesiastical politicians exploiting sacramental theology. From this perspective, Stoddard's actual doctrine of the Lord's Supper was the product of a long series of discussions among continental and English theologians. Though it was indeed a response to specific colonial problems, the Stoddardean controversy also reflected the cosmopolitan character of Puritan concerns in late seventeenth-century New England.[11]

As the controversy gathered heat, both Increase Mather and Edward Taylor used arguments against Stoddard that George Gillespie, Richard Baxter, and Stephen Charnock used decades earlier against Prynne, Humphrey, and Timson. As to when Stoddard's views came to the attention of the wider church community, it has been suggested[12] that Increase Mather preached an election sermon in Boston on May 23, 1677, and though he did not mention Stoddard by name, he most likely had him in mind as the "Teacher" who was beginning to modify the Synod of 1662's requirement for participation in the Lord's Supper. "I wish there be not Teachers found in our Israel, that have espoused loose, large Principles here, designing to bring all persons to the Lord's Supper, who have an Historical Faith, and are not scandalous in life, although

---

10. Charles Randolph Coney suggests that it was Stoddard's tutor at Harvard, Jonathan Mitchel (1624–1668), who was a key influence in introducing his students to the thoughts of Thomas Erastus and John Humphrey as well as the writings of the Scottish Presbyterian Samuel Rutherford, who also rejected the notion of limiting church membership to the visible saints. Coney, 40–41. Also, see Coffman, 35–38; Foxcroft, "A Letter to the Author," 338 – 341.

11. Holifield, *Intellectual Sources*, 392.

12. Davis, *Edward Taylor vs. Solomon Stoddard*, 4.

they never had Experience of a work of Regeneration on their Souls."[13] Herein lay Mather's chief disagreement with Stoddardism.

It may have been John Russell of Hadley[14] who put Mather onto this development in Stoddard's thought, as the former was not a firm supporter of the Synod of 1662 and would have been extremely sensitive to further liberalizing the covenant. Also, Russell's church was in Hadley, just across the Connecticut River to the east of Stoddard in Northampton.

Tracking the development of Stoddardism is not an easy task due to the lack of extant material and the evolutionary nature of Stoddard's ideas. The earliest formal articulation of Stoddardism was contained in a pamphlet published in 1679 entitled *Nine Arguments Against Examinations Concerning the Work of Grace Before Admission to the Lords Supper*. Stoddard's central proposition upon which he based all of his arguments was: "All Such as do make a Solemn Profession of Faith, & Repentance, & are of Godly Conversation, having Knowledge to Examine themselves, & discern the Lords Body, are to be admitted to the Lords Supper."[15]

Stoddard went on to explain that "a Profession of Faith, & Repentance" was not an admission of saving faith as much as an assent to the historical Christian faith. He also said that "Godly Conversation" meant that a person was striving to live according to "all the Commandments, not living in the Presence of any known Sin, or Omission of any Duty." Thus a visible saint was one who professed a faith in Jesus Christ and lived a morally upright life in accordance with the commands of Scripture, even though he or she could not point to an experience of regeneration.

Then in true Ramist style,[16] he responded to the question: "What is that Knowledge to examine themselves & discern the Lords Body?" He

---

13. Increase Mather, *A Discourse Concerning the Danger of Apostasy*. A sermon preached in Boston on May 23, 1677. Quoted in Davis, *Taylor vs. Stoddard*, 4.

14. Miller cites that Russell sent Increase Mather a letter in March of 1681 saying, "Our good brother Stoddard hath bin strenuously promoting his position concerning that right which persons sound in doctrine of faith, & of (as he calls it) a holy Conversation, haue come to full Communion." Miller, *Mind*, 232.

15. Quoted in Davis, *Taylor vs. Stoddard*, 67.

16. The Ramist method was a kind of logic made popular by French educator and Protestant martyr Peter Ramus (1515–1572). It was used most exclusively by the first two generations of Puritan writers and preachers. Miller, *Mind*, 12.

claimed that discerning the Lord's Body was an individual's responsibility to recognize God's work in his or her own heart and not the responsibility of the clergy or congregation to determine whether the person was regenerate. Stoddard then laid out his arguments:

> Ans: 1. Knowledge to examine a mans Selfe, is knowledge of those things he ought to examine himselfe about, viz, Faith, Repentance, Love, New Obedience. What the nature of them is: & Competently to distinguish False Grace, from true.

> Ans: 2. Knowledge to Discern the Lords Body is a knowledge of the Nature, Necessity, & Use of the Lords Supper.

> Arg: 1. They that are Visible Saints, & walke as Such are to be admitted to the Lords Supper; if they have knowledge to examine themselves, & discern the Lords Body. Such Persons are the visible heirs of Salvation. Salvation is peculiar unto Saints, Heb. 12.14, Matt. 7.22 & when persons are thus qualified we ought to look on them as visible heirs of Salvation. If such be not visible Saints, then having been in church from their Infancy, they ought to be ejected. Its an horrible corruption for the church to [admit] such as not visible Saints.

> Arg: 2. Such Qualifications as were sufficient in adult persons in order to Communion in all ordinances in the Jewish Church, are sufficient with the addition of knowledge to examine themselves, & discern the Lords Body, in order to such Communion in the Gospell Church.

> Arg: 3. Those that are Qualified for Church membership are Qualified for Full Communion, if they have knowledge to examine themselves, & discern the Lords Body.

> Arg: 4. Those who do Syncerely make that Profession which the Church is built upon, are to be admitted to the Lords Supper, if they have knowledge to examine themselves, & discern the Lords Body.

> Arg: 6: Such as are fit to be Baptized, are fit likewise for the Lords Supper, if they have the knowledge to Examine themselves, & discern the Lords Body. Because Baptism is a Sacrament for the strengthening, & Confirming of a Faith, as well as the Lords Supper. Those that were qualified for Circumcision, were qualified

for Passover. When Children come to be Adults they are reputed to be Believers, or Unbelievers: not according to the Stock they come from, but according to what they Profess, & the nature of their Carriage. Because such Persons do bring forth fruits of Faith; they can't be denied to be visible Believers who bring forth fruits of Faith, Matt. 7.15.

Arg: 9. Those that are fit to be Confirmed Members of the Church, are fit for the Lords Supper.[17]

Edward Taylor of Westfield, MA, preached a Foundation Sermon in 1679, which hallmarked his loyalty to the orthodox views of the Puritan founders. It was based upon Eph 2:22, and his main point was that a particular church was the dwelling place of God, which made it holy and necessitated that the stones (individual members) that composed the house must also be holy. "It is necessary that a Person seeking with any Church of Christ to have Communion, give an account of the workings of God's Spirit upon his heart."[18]

Taylor's comments on limiting admission to the Lord's Supper to those who could give a "relation" of God's work in their hearts was most likely aimed at his Northampton neighbor Solomon Stoddard. This provides some evidence that Stoddardism began by extending the half-way measures to include the Lord's Supper as well as Baptism, and eliminating the requirement for a public relation of regeneration. Thomas Davis goes on to say: "There is, however, nothing in the [Taylor's] sermon which would suggest that the view of the Sacrament as a converting ordinance or of . . . [Presbyterian] church polity . . . are at this point part of the proposed changes ascribed to Stoddard. The first stage of Stoddard's developing views . . . involves only a desire to modify half-way practices. Nor is there any evidence . . . which would suggest that Stoddard made any changes in the actual practice of the Northampton Church."[19]

However, the relative obscurity of Stoddardism was soon to be brought out into the open. In 1679, eighteen ministers including Solomon Stoddard and Increase Mather petitioned the General Court to order a synod which would propose measures of reformation. The

17. Davis, *Taylor vs. Stoddard*, 68–81.

18. Taylor, *Church Records and Related Sermons*, 128.

19. Davis, *Taylor vs. Stoddard*, 8.

shock of the bloody King Phillip's War (1675–1676)[20] along with declining membership rates in the churches alarmed the clergy and convinced them that something needed to be done to encourage reformation and revival. The Synod was convened on September 10, 1679, in Boston, "for the revisal of the platform of discipline agreed upon by the churches, 1647,[21] and what else may appear necessary for the preventing of schisms, haeresies, prophaneness, & the establishment of the churches in one faith & order of the gospell."[22]

The Reforming Synod of 1679 was only the third synod called by the Massachusetts General Court under the old charter (annulled on October 23, 1684). The first had been the Synod at Cambridge, which had produced the Cambridge Platform of 1648. The second synod had been in 1662, which had resulted in what has been called "The Half-Way Covenant." The third and final synod was called for the purpose of answering two questions drafted by Increase Mather: "What are the evils that have provoked the Lord to bring his judgment on New England?"; "What is to be done so that these evils may be reformed?"[23]

There was a general awareness that God's judgment was upon New England for its moral and spiritual decline. This awareness was due not only to King Phillip's War, but also to a series of natural catastrophes (like the Boston fire of 1676, which burned most of the buildings in town including Increase Mather's church), a rash of poor harvests, an economic downturn in trade, an increasing toleration of heresy (like Quakerism), a growing anti-clergy sentiment, and the threat of the loss of the Bay Colony's charter with England.

---

20. The immediate cause of this conflict was the hanging of three men in June 1675 convicted of killing a man named John Sassamon, who, only weeks before, had warned the governor of the Plymouth Colony of King Phillip's plan to wage war against the settlers. The three hanged were Wampanoag Indians loyal to Phillip, the *sachem* (chief or king) of the Wampanoags, also known by his Algonquin name Metacom or Metacomet. In response to these hangings, Phillip began to attack English towns (Northampton on March 14, 1676) and for fourteen months what ensued has been called the bloodiest war in American history. Phillip was killed on August 12, 1676. Lepore, *The Name of War*, xi.

21. The Cambridge Platform was not revised at the Synod, but affirmed along with the doctrinal position of the Savoy Declaration (1658), a modification of the Westminster Confession (1646) to fit the congregational polity of English Congregationalists.

22. Walker, *Creeds and Platform*, 415.

23. Gildrie, *The Profane, the Civil, and the Godly*, 20.

Perry Miller observes that while "the fast-day" sermon, which was usually preached annually on the days of political elections, was characteristic of the first generation of Puritans, the "jeremiad" was the dominant literary form of the second generation.[24] This type of sermon stressed the importance of the covenant, and would usually pronounce the failures of that generation to live up to covenant prescriptions. These denunciations would often use the prophetic texts of Isaiah or Jeremiah (thus, *jeremiad*), and would be followed by appeals for repentance and reformation. The document produced by the Reforming Synod of 1679 read like an extensive jeremiad.[25]

In response to the first question about the evils that provoked the Lord to bring his judgments on New England, the following were listed in expanded form: "a visible decay of godliness, abounding pride, the name of God has been polluted and profaned by oath-taking and imprecations, Sabbath-breaking, growing ignorance of Scripture, intemperance and a lack of modesty, promise-breaking, inordinate affection for worldly things, opposition to the work of reformation, a self-centered lack of concern for the social good, a lack of repentance and faith or sins against the Gospel."[26]

In response to the second question about what should be done to bring about reformation, there were thirteen solutions offered. It was solution three that pinpointed the conflict between Mather and Stoddard. "It is requisite that Persons be not admitted into Communion in the Lords Supper, without making a personal and publick profession of Faith and Repentance, either orally, or in some other way, so as shall be to the just satisfaction of the Church; and that therefore both Elders and Churches be duly watchful and circumspect in this matter, 1 Cor. 11. 28, 29. Acts 2. 41, 42. Ezek. 44. 7, 8, 9."[27]

Solomon Stoddard was not unknown to the ministers who attended the Synod of 1679. Miller indicates that Stoddard had been the first to become aware of the potential problem with King Phillip and had sent a warning to Boston, adding a rebuke when he heard that the magistrates were not going to send protection to the towns of the Connecticut

---

24. Miller, *Mind*, 29.
25. Hardman, *The Spiritual Awakeners*, 31.
26. Smith, 205–212.
27. Ibid., 213.

Valley.[28] While Increase Mather was aware of Stoddard's position on polity and secular affairs, he may not have been aware of Stoddard's forcefulness and ability to debate his position on just about anything.

There arose an issue at the Synod concerning one of the evils which was believed to have provoked the judgment of God on New England. Ralph Wheelocke, a wealthy farmer and a deputy to the General Court, suggested that such an evil might be that ministers and magistrates had not been paying as much tax as everyone else. Stoddard raged at old Wheelocke and accused him of being a liar. The next day, Wheelocke apologized and Stoddard had everyone's attention.[29]

Stoddard also locked horns with Mather on many of his proposals, and as was already mentioned, especially on the wording of solution three. Mather had proposed that the Lord's Supper be open to all who could give a relation of God's saving work in their hearts. The issue was so hotly debated that Urian Oakes, who was appointed moderator, managed to defer discussion and push for a vote. The Synod decided to go with Stoddard's wording that required persons taking the Lord's Supper to make "a personal and publick profession of Faith and Repentance."[30] This is how Stoddard remembered the whole affair twenty years later:

> Some of the Elders in the Synod had drawn up a Conclusion, That persons should make a relation of the work of God's Spirit upon their hearts, in order to come into full Communion. Some others of the Elders objected against it, and after some discourse it was agreed to have a dispute on that question, Whether those Professors of Religion as are of good Conversation, are not to be admitted to full Communion, provided they are able to Examine themselves, and discern the Lords body. Mr. Mather held the negative; I laboured to make good the Affirmative; the result was, That they blotted out that clause of Making a Relation of the work of Gods Spirit and put in the room of it, The Making a Profession of their Faith and Repentance; and so I Voted with the Rest, and am of the same judgment still.[31]

Each man went home from the Synod believing he had won the day. Mather interpreted the language to reflect his meaning of testifying

28. Christensen, "Pope or Persuader," 112–113.

29. Miller, *Mind*, 230.

30. Gildrie, 34.

31. Stoddard, *An Appeal*, 93–94.

to the experience of saving grace, while Stoddard believed that it refer-
enced one's agreeing to the covenant.[32] Also, either during or after the
Synod, Stoddard apparently gave Mather a manuscript of his proposals
regarding open Communion, which Mather used in his "Confutation"
of Stoddard's position published in 1680.[33]

The Synod then made the recommendation that individual churches should take the responsibility to fix certain times for covenant renewal
ceremonies, where church members could recommit themselves to the
covenant of their founders or create their own type of covenant commitment. Perry Miller points out that this practice had already found
its way into some churches prior to 1675.[34] However, after the Synod of
1679, church covenant renewals multiplied in popularity as a means of
drawing younger folks into church membership.

> Like the Half-Way Covenant, covenant renewal ceremonies
> functioned more like recruiting devices to draw the rising gen-
> eration into the churches on Sunday than as engines of conver-
> sion. But covenant renewal did not end with corporate pledges.
> Rather, ministers employed the occasion to inaugurate a period
> of intensely conversionist preaching whose goal was "revival"—a
> time when large numbers of the rising generation would come
> into full membership at once. All regular preaching treated salva-
> tion themes, but in periods of revival the "New Birth" received
> concentrated attention. These periods were a "season" of weeks
> and even months during which time many adult "children" and
> half-way members were converted and became full members.
> Most ministers could count on such dramatic returns only once
> or twice in their preaching careers, when the combined factors
> of covenant renewal, conversionist preaching, and a large pool
> of eligible candidates (adult children mid- to late- twenties) con-
> verged to produce an influx of new members.[35]

Although Increase Mather may have been the "brains" behind the
Reforming Synod and the first to lead his church in a covenant renewal,
it was Solomon Stoddard who became the "soul" behind the Synod and
the most effective revivalist of that generation.[36] In the course of his fifty-

32. Miller, *Mind*, 232.
33. Davis, *Taylor vs. Stoddard*, 8.
34. Ibid., 116.
35. Stout, 98.
36. Hardman, 36.

eight year ministry, he saw five special seasons of revival "harvests": in 1679, 1683, 1696, 1712, and 1718.[37] "Where did Stoddard get the idea of "harvests," or revivals? He derived it from the history of the Christian church, which had frequently experienced awakenings over centuries. The Puritans, ever zealous students of Scripture, looked to sections such as Psalm 85:6 ('Wilt thou not revive us again, that my people may rejoice in thee?') as injunctions to pray for the renewing of believers. The absence of revivals, as in Increase Mather's experience, was cause for great distress and searching of the soul."[38]

Apparently the numbers of people converted in Stoddard's harvests were unmatched anywhere in New England up to that time.[39] In fact, Stoddard was such an effective evangelist that Increase Mather even wrote a forward to Stoddard's book *A Guide to Christ* and recommended it to his students in the ministry.[40] Also, the esteemed itinerant evangelist of the next generation, George Whitefield, mentioned Stoddard's book in his journal in an entry dated October 17, 1740: "After a little refreshment, we crossed the ferry to Northampton, where no less than three hundred souls were saved about five years ago. Their pastor's name is Edwards, successor and grandson to the great Stoddard, whose memory will always be precious to my soul, and whose books entitled *A Guide to Christ*, and *Safety of Appearing in Christ's Righteousness*, I would recommend to all."[41]

When he returned from the Synod, Stoddard led his congregation in covenant renewal and preached a twenty-three week series on Joshua's renewal of the covenant in Josh 24:14-24. He followed that with a series on conversion from Ps 23. All of this led to his first "harvest" and his revivalist preaching is here exemplified from some unpublished sermon notes. "[As] in the body there are the seeds of all naturall diseases, so in the souls are the seeds of all spiritual diseases . . . as it is with a man that has consumption, he is not laid up but walks to work a little. But he is

---

37. An argument could be made for six harvests, if the smaller revival of 1727 is included in which the young Edwards participated while Stoddard's associate. See Edwards, "Memoirs," xxxviii.

38. Hardman, 34. Perry Miller calls Stoddard not only "the first great 'revivalist' in New England" but also the one who "inaugurated the era of revivalism on the American frontier." (Miller, "Solomon Stoddard," 316–319.)

39. Jonathan Edwards, "A Faithful Narrative," 232.

40. Stout, 99.

41. Whitefield, *Journals*, 476.

in a very pining condition. So sometimes is the soul of a godly man. He is in a withering estate . . . his distemper may prevaile so dreadfully that he can't make an acceptable prayer, can't sanctify a Sabbath, can't do any such service as he was wont to do in an acceptable manner unto God. His corruption . . . ha[s] such power as to render him unserviceable."[42]

Stoddard then offered Christ to his hearers. Christ would become the "physician" to his covenant elect, if they would open their hearts to him in utter dependence. Stoddard, the preacher, would always press his hearers for a commitment and was not one to urge his hearers merely to content themselves with covenant faithfulness and duty. [43]

Though evangelistically driven, Solomon Stoddard was a thorough-going Calvinist who believed in the doctrine of election and the depravity of humanity. He was utterly convinced that no one could save himself by his own goodness, by trusting in an historical faith, or by his religious affections. The sinner needed to become convinced of the "badness of his own heart."

> When men see the badness of their own hearts, they are ready to be discouraged; but they are in a more hopeful condition than before. If men are strangers to their own hearts, they will trust in themselves and neglect Christ. God reveals the excellency of Christ to them. Men will never come to Christ until they are convinced what corrupt, blind, and dead creatures they are. And, therefore, the more God shows him the badness of his heart, the more graciously He deals with him. The badness of the heart is a matter of sorrow, but the sight of that badness is a matter of encouragement. The more they see of that, the more hope there is of their being prepared for Christ.[44]

Stoddard, however, believed that this humiliation was not the first step of conversion, but merely a part of the preparation for conversion. It should be remembered that Stoddard and the Puritan Founders (with the possible exception of John Cotton) uniformly agreed that while human ability has no place in conversion, a person must be "prepared" before faith and conversion took place. Yet these men also believed that such preparation was a part of man's natural state. In fact, in the pref-

---

42. Stout, 101. (Stout is indebted to Thomas M. Davis for sharing his transcript of Stoddard's sermon on Ps 23:3 from which this quote was taken.)

43. Ibid., 100.

44. Stoddard, *Guide to Christ*, 29.

ace of Stoddard's *A Guide to Christ*, he mentioned the likes of Perkins, Sibbes, Preston, Hooker, Shepherd, and Norton as all supporting the necessity of preparation. At the very foundation of Stoddard's doctrine of conversion was the understanding that the unregenerate sinner can do something to prepare for his conversion. Stoddard, along with Thomas Hooker, believed that there were two steps of preparation: conviction and humiliation. "There are two degrees of this preparation: the first is Awakening, whereby the sinner is convinced of a present necessity of peace and reconciliation with God; whereby he is put upon a diligent use of all means in order to his salvation: the other is Humiliation, whereby the sinner is brought out of himself, and off from his carnal confidences, to yield himself a Prisoner to God: until the soul be humbled as he is not capable of faith."[45]

There was no progressive movement from nature to grace in Stoddard's thought as claimed by more liberal Boston men like Briant, Gay, and Chauncy. For Stoddard, there was a great divide between the natural man and the converted one. There was no process that drove a darkened sinner to become an enlightened saint. "For Stoddard faith was not a process; it was a constellation of graces, given at once. Stoddard said that faith was a condition of justification, but it almost seems as if he was making a play on words. Faith was more the condition one is in when one is justified than it is the condition by which one is justified. He spoke of justification as conditional upon faith; but only God sets the condition, he alone fulfills it."[46]

Stoddard was careful to instruct those who ministered to persons in such a state of humiliation that they should not be given any false hope or encouragement.[47] "Yet there is no ground to hope that, until he thoroughly sees himself, he will accept the offer of the gospel. Men must first be humble before they will believe. Invitations to come to Christ will never be successful until men are driven out of their false refuges."[48]

45. Stoddard, *Safety of Appearing*, 205.

46. Jones, 115.

47. "*A Guide to Christ* appeared just as [Jonathan] Edward's ministerial generation was entering upon theological training, and it was reprinted in 1735, when the revival in the Connecticut Valley was at its height. *The Safety of Appearing*, in many respects Stoddard's finest work on conversion, was reprinted in 1729, when his death would put many in mind of his career, and again in 1742, at the height of the Great Awakening." Schafer, *Theology of Revival*, 333.

48. Stoddard, *Guide*, 30.

Therefore, at the foundation of Stoddard's understanding of conversion was the work of preparation. "There is an absolute necessity in nature, that men be prepared before the Exercise of Faith; men cannot exercise Faith, till the heart be prepared by a sense of danger, and the insufficiency of other things."[49] While this preparation is a part of common grace, it has no part in converting grace. Stoddard believed that the unconverted sinner must strive to the utmost of his ability not to earn salvation, but to show his own unregenerate heart the "experience of the failing of all means."[50] This unconverted person must be urged to reform so he can experience the humiliation that he does not have the ability to reform. "They are to be urged to Reformation. . . . For the neglect of Reformation will put a stop to the work, & they will not get forward in the work of Humiliation, till they are Reformed; as the first Concoction prepares for the second, so Reformation does for Humiliation . . . he that will not part with sinful practices, will not yield himself into the hands of Justice."[51]

Humiliation, therefore, is the condition in which a sinner is absolutely convinced that there is nothing he can do to save himself, nor is there anything within himself that is worth saving. In addition, Stoddard stressed that there is no difference between the humiliation of the elect and the non-elect except for the end results.

> As there may be no difference in the voyages of two ships for a pretty while, one of which at last arrives in the harbor, and the other is cast away, so it is here. Those that shall never be converted may have the same experiences for a considerable time that those have who shall be converted. There may be no difference in their awakenings, in their reformations, in their temptations, in their encouragements, nor in respect of their frames. This appears: 1. Because those strivings that men may have who shall never be converted are sufficient to bring men forward towards Christ. There is no necessity at all that the elect should have any strivings, for a time, than what are common to reprobates. The convictions that reprobates may have are sufficient to bring men forward towards Christ. 2. They who are converted are not capable of any strivings of the Spirit, but what are common until they come to be humbled and to believe. It is a pretty while after God

49. Ibid., xix.

50. Stoddard, *Safety*, 103.

51. Stoddard, *Guide*, xix.

begins to strive with the elect, before they come to be humbled, and believe in Christ; and before that, they are not capable of any strivings but what are common.[52]

This blurring of the lines of election undergirded Stoddard's argument against anyone ultimately knowing the identity of the elect and non-elect, and consequently against establishing a pure church made up of the visible elect. As has been mentioned, Stoddard was a thorough Calvinist, but he had what Miller calls a "stark conception of irrational sovereignty."[53] Stoddard acknowledged that when someone underwent the work of conversion, he was subject to a lot of discouraging temptations as to whether he was of the elect or not.

One temptation is that he is not elected; that God has overlooked him and appointed him to condemnation. This sometimes lies upon the heart with great weight. In this case he may be told:

1. That those things that make him fear that he is not elected are no certain signs of it. There are no certain tokens of reprobation upon him. Those things he takes to be signs are very uncertain. The greatness of his sins do not argue reprobation. Many who have been guilty of great sins have been elected.

2. That it is a sinful thing for him to draw any conclusion about his election. It is a secret reserved in God's own breast, and he cannot determine anything understandably about it. Deuteronomy 29:29, "secret things belong unto the Lord our God." When he undertakes to conclude that he is not elected, he acts presumptuously.

3. That God's striving with him by His Spirit is a hopeful sign that he is elected . . . the more earnestly the man follows after God and labors to get into a converted condition, the more hopeful it is that God has elected him, for where God has appointed the end, He has appointed the means also.[54]

Stoddard was not playing "fast and loose" with the concept of election, but he was stressing his belief that God is absolutely free to choose upon whom to bestow mercy. "God is the Author of conversion. Men must be born of the Spirit. Whatever means are used will be ineffective if there is not the operation of the Spirit. . . . And the way wherein He

52. Ibid., 39–40.
53. Miller, *Mind*, 235.
54. Stoddard, *Guide*, 9–10.

does it is by letting spiritual light into the soul, by irradiating the mind, letting in beams of light into the heart. In that way God increases grace, and in that way He gives grace at first. While men remain in darkness they remain in the kingdom of darkness, but by enlightening the mind He changes the heart. It is by inward discoveries of the glory of God that He sanctifies the heart."[55]

Stoddard also believed that God is not only absolutely free in conversion but He is also irresistibly glorious when He is known.[56]

> God is so glorious that if he is known the heart will be drawn to him. Psalm 30:7: "Because of the excellency of Thy loving kindness, the children of men put their trust in the shadow of Thy wings." The excellency of God draws the heart irresistibly to Him when it is known. The knowledge of God is inseparable from holiness. All who know Him are holy. The very capacity to know God makes men capable of being holy, of loving Him and trusting Him. . . . Hell fire will not purge away men's dross. One glimpse of the glory of God will do more than all the punishments in the world to make men holy. When men see the glory of God, they would be acting against their nature if they should not be holy. . . . When men know the excellency of God, they must choose Him. The glory of God is such that it captivates the heart; where it is seen it has magnetic power; it irresistibly conquers the will. There is a necessity of loving God when He is seen.[57]

Stoddard added one more very unique aspect to this picture of God's absolute freedom to reveal Himself to anyone and His absolute irresistibility once He is revealed. Stoddard believed that man has the ability of beholding God's glory even before he is regenerated.

> Man, in his natural estate, is represented in Scripture as utterly depraved, dead in trespasses and sins. He is blind and in darkness. It may be thought that he is incapable of seeing the gloriousness of God until there is first a habitual change in his understanding; but if we examine the Word of God we may find plain intimations that this light precedes habitual change. John 5:25: "The time is coming, and now is, when the dead shall hear the voice of the Son of God; and they that hear shall live." Hearing

---

55. Stoddard, *The Nature of Saving Conversion*, 26.

56. "The irresistible working of God has been shifted from the sovereignty of his absolute power to the irresistible nature of his aesthetic attraction. The similarity to Edwards is obvious." Jones, 109.

57. Stoddard, *Conversion*, 27–29.

the voice of Christ is antecedent to their living. It is in that way
that life enters upon them. 2 Corinthians 3:18: "We all with open
face beholding as in a glass the glory of the Lord are changed into
the same image." Before they are changed into God's image, they
behold His glory. This makes it evident that men are capable of
beholding the glory of the Lord before the habitual change.[58]

Stoddard was quick to clarify that this capability or inclination to
see God's glory is not the same thing as having a natural power or ability
to know God. "A faculty of understanding instructed and assisted by
the Spirit must enable men to know God."[59] And this divine enablement
flows out of the mercy of God wherein He is willing to deal graciously
with His creatures. Even here Stoddard made sure it was understood
that the merciful purposes of God do not flow from a merciful nature
but from His sovereign will.

The merciful purposes of God were the free acting of his own
will. God was an absolute free agent, either to bestow mercy or
deny it as he pleased: if he had naturally an inclination to shew
mercy, he could not have forborn to shew mercy without going
contrary to the inclinations of his own heart. The exercise of
mercy does not flow necessarily from the merciful nature of God;
but he exercises grace freely from his sovereign will and pleasure:
there is nothing in God's nature that does compel him to shew
mercy to any man. . . . There are voluntary inclinations in God to
shew mercy, but no natural inclinations.[60]

One can see how Stoddard's emphasis on God's absolute freedom
and irresistibility would cause him to rebuff the notion that anyone
would claim to know who the truly elect were so as to bestow upon them
church membership and the right to receive the Lord's Supper. On the
other hand, one can also see how some might find in Stoddard's thought
the latent seeds of Arminianism.

But we may ask, is this not crypto-Arminianism, an unduly op-
timistic view of fallen man's ability? Not at all, answers Stoddard,
who holds uncompromisingly with Calvin that man is morally
depraved and utterly impotent. Man as created possessed a regard to his own welfare, a natural self-love which as such was

58. Ibid., 31.
59. Ibid., 32.
60. Stoddard, *Safety*, 10.

good; it was kept in its proper place by the higher principles of righteousness and love to God. But the latter were lost in the fall, and now an exorbitant self-love, out of control, dominates man completely. So complete has been the degeneration that now even the best of unconverted men are sworn enemies to God's wisdom, power, and justice, "yea, to the very being of God." [61]

Thus it was Stoddard's view of evangelism and his morphology of preparation that set his understanding of the Lord's Supper in its proper context. His main concern was not to maintain a pure church, but to convert the unconverted. "Stoddard was more concerned with making the church and the sacraments into effective evangelical instruments than he was with preserving the past." [62] In fact, it was unique to Solomon Stoddard within the New England context that he viewed the Lord's Supper as a part of the preparation for conversion. [63]

> The Lords Supper is Instituted to be a means of Regeneration, it is not appointed for the Converting of Men to the Christian Religion, for only such as are Converted may partake of it; but it is not only for the Strengthening of Saints, but a means also to work Saving Regeneration. This Ordinance hath a proper tendency to draw sinners to Christ; in this Ordinance there is a particular invitation to sinners, to come to Christ for Pardon, here is an affecting Representation of the Virtue of Christ's sufferings, here is a Seal whereby the Truth of the Gospel is confirmed, all which are very proper to draw sinners to Christ. [64]

Stoddard's views were subject to much misunderstanding, in part because his "opponents" (such as Increase Mather and Edward Taylor) took what he said as a profound deviation from the Puritan Fathers and a veritable threat to the future of the New England Way. [65] Mather

61. Schafer, *Theology of Revival*, 336.

62. Jones, 113.

63. Schafer, *Theology of Revival*, 340.

64. Stoddard, *The Doctrine of Instituted Churches*, 22.

65. The principal titles (in full) in the controversy with Increase Mather, arranged chronologically, were: Stoddard, *Inexcusableness of Neglecting the Worship of God, Under a Pretence of Being in an Unconverted Condition.* This was a sermon given in 1707 and published in 1708. Increase Mather, *A Dissertation wherein the Strange Doctrine Lately Published in a Sermon, The Tendency of which Is, to Encourage Unsanctified Persons (While Such) to Approach the Holy Table of the Lord, Is Examined and Confuted.* This was published in 1708. Stoddard, *An Appeal to the Learned, Being a Vindication of the Right of Visible Saints to the Lord's Supper, though They Be Destitute of a Saving Work*

went so far as to accuse Stoddard of bordering on Roman Catholicism. There is even a hint that Taylor (and possibly Edwards) saw in Stoddard's thought the seeds of Arminianism.[66]

However, much of the misunderstanding of his thought also occurred because of Stoddard's inexactness and "lack of precision in his theological vocabulary."[67] His claim that the Lord's Supper was a "means of Regeneration and not of Conversion" merely meant that Communion was a preparatory work that preceded conversion and not the means of conversion itself. While this view did not preclude that conversion might take place at the Table (as happened in his own experience), it did mean that the Lord's Supper was not a vehicle of sacramental regeneration.[68]

It should be remembered that it was Increase Mather and Edward Taylor who first accused Stoddard of holding a view of the Lord's Supper as a converting ordinance and opening the Table to pagans, whores, thieves, etc.[69] They added their own meaning to his position. Stoddard denied advocating that Communion was open to anyone regardless of their life and profession. The Lord's Supper was open to all church members: those who were visible saints on the basis of professing faith in Christ and striving to live a godly life. "Visible Saints are such as make a serious profession of the true religion, together with those that do descend from them, till rejected of God."[70] As to the criticism that he viewed the Lord Supper as a converting ordinance, James Walsh observes:

> He had maintained consistently for years that the Lord's Supper was a converting ordinance just in the way that all other church ordinances were. A good sermon, for example, "stirs up a principle of Grace where it is . . . and there be a generating Power in the Gospel." Baptism, too, had "a real influence into salvation." (*The*

---

*of God's Spirit on Their Hearts, Against the Exceptions of Mr. Increase Mather.* This was published as a pamphlet in 1709.

66. Walsh, 112; Grabo, "Edward Taylor's Treatise," 129.

67. Coney, 60.

68. Granted the language of Stoddard's sermon on Galatians 3:1 would seem to contradict this assertion, but careful examination reveals that his view of Communion as "tis usefull unto Saints and its usefull to make men Saints" is a far cry from a view of sacramental regeneration. See Walsh, "Open Communion," 111; also Haroutunian, *Piety versus Moralism,* 97–98. Haroutunian accepts Mather's contention that Stoddard had embraced the *opus operatum* doctrine of the Roman Catholics.

69. Grabo, 80.

70. Stoddard, *Instituted Churches,* 6.

*Safety of Appearing*, 143). This is all Stoddard had ever meant when he spoke of the Communion as a converting ordinance. He tried to make this crystal clear in 1707 when he pointed out that "The giving of Converting Grace is not limited to any one Ordinance." (*The Inexcusableness of Neglecting the Worship of God*, 17). Stoddard also realized at this time that he should make clear his belief that whatever converting potential the sacrament contained was limited to visible saints. This would make more credible his exclusion of the unbaptized and of notorious sinners from church membership. Stoddard therefore declared flatly that the Lord's Supper could convert visible saints, but that "The Hearing of the Word only is the appointed means for the Conversion of others" (*The Inexcusableness of Neglecting the Worship of God*, 28).[71]

Once again, Stoddard's main concern was not to create a pure church, but to convert the unconverted. He crafted an evangelical theology which was based upon the preaching of the Gospel and viewed the Lord's Supper as another form of "preaching" that Gospel and converting sinners.[72] In his sermon on Gal 3:1, which he preached to his congregation on October 5, 1690, we find a mature articulation of what he meant by the Lord's Supper as a converting ordinance.[73]

> Its universally acknowledg'd that the Lords Supper is for the Strengthening, & encrease of Grace. But all are not so well satisfied that its for the begetting of Grace. But the Dissatisfaction arises more for the want of an impartiall enquiry, than from any obscurity in the thing itselfe. As the Passover of old was, the Lords Supper now is appointed for Conversion. Sometimes it is blessed by God for this end: & its design'd by God for this end. It is singularly usefull unto saints to quicken, & encourage them & make them fruitfull. But the use of it is Confin'd within too narrow bounds: 'tis usefull unto Saints: & its usefull also to make men Saints. There are two greate Ends of the Lords Supper. One is to shew forth the Death of Christ, 1 Cor. 11.26: to ac-

---

71. Walsh, 111.

72. De Arteaga, *Forgotten Power*, 75. De Arteaga calls Stoddard's view "Sacramental Evangelicalism."

73. "It has been assumed that Stoddard's open advocacy of the converting nature of the Lord's Supper began at some point following the change in 1677 in his method of keeping church records. . . . Taylor's copy of the 'Arguments' demonstrates that as late as 1688, Stoddard had not yet adopted the more extreme position [of the Lord's Supper as a converting ordinance]." Davis, "Solomon Stoddard's Arguments," 80.

knowledge before the World the Saving Efficacy of the Death of Christ. The other is our Spirituall benefit, as well as Conversion, as Edification of them that are Converted. The same arguments that nourish Faith do beget it.

Conversion is taken two wayes in the Scripture. Sometimes its taken for the Conversion to the Christian Religion. Acts 15.3. Declaring the Conversion of the Gentiles. And Participation in the Lords Supper is not appointed to the work of this Conversion: but the building up of them that are already converted to the Christian Religion. . . . But sometimes Conversion is taken for a Saving Turning of the Soul unto God, & Participation in the Lords Supper is a means to procure this. This Ordinance as well as others is a means to make up the match between Christ, & the Soul. It has Spirituall influence into mans Conversion.[74]

Stoddard believed along with most of Puritan clergy that the Lord's Supper was for spiritual growth in grace for those who were already converted. While this was an important use of the sacrament, to Stoddard there was another. Communion was also useful to those who were not yet converted. He clearly stated that by conversion he did not mean from outside the church to the Christian religion, since this type of unbeliever would never be allowed to take the Lord's Supper in his church. As has already been mentioned, Stoddard believed that while "the Hearing of the Word only is the appointed means for the Conversion of others,"[75] it is the Lord's Supper that could convert only the visible saints. The following explanation forms the very basis of understanding Stoddard's entire system of open Communion.

If the Lords Supper be only for the strengthening of grace and not for the begetting of it, then men must know that they are converted before they come to the Lords Supper. Upon this supposition they must forbeare coming to the Lord Supper until they know their conversion & everytime that they lose the knowledge of their conversion; don't argue that they must forbeare every time they have scruples about their conversion, for a man may have scruples about it & yet know it, but ignorant of it makes it unlawfull. . . .

[Rather] The Lords Supper is open to all visible believers that are not scandalous & can examine themselves & discern the Lords body; if men live wickedly they are not to be admit-

74. Davis, *Taylor vs. Stoddard*, 132.
75. Stoddard, *Inexcusableness*, 28.

ted to the Lord Supper tho' that be a converting ordinance; if they be Church members God hath appointed the censures of the Church for their conversion: other special ordinances are appointed for such, & not the Lords Supper. . . . [The Lord's Supper can be useful as an] awakening to them that have come often to the Lords Supper & yet are not converted. . . .

[Do] not be backward to admit orderly professors to the Lords Supper, tho' you may fear they are not savingly converted. Men have need of all the helpes that God hath sanctified in order to their conversion, the devil tryes: & we had need to use all means to forward their conversion out of a respect unto the name and kingdome of God, & out of a respect unto them. Many of them are your children & kindred: you should doe whatever you can to advance this worke & if this doctrine be true you ought to accept them unto a participation in this ordinance. I speak not a word for men of loose carriage, I wish you were more strict than you are with respect to them; but be not backward to accept of such as have good conversation, dont say you fear that they are unregenerate, for if so, they may have more need to come. The Apostles readily accepted those that made a profession of the gospel: be not you overscrupulous & difficult: dont discourage them from coming . . . dont hang back and shew an unwilling spirit to accept of them, dont clog their admissions with any needless impositions.[76]

Opening Communion to all visible saints,[77] whether proven regenerate or not, was Stoddard's evangelical method of casting the gospel net as wide as possible, thus preparing as many souls as possible to come into contact with the grace of God. Elsewhere, Stoddard claimed that preaching the Gospel itself was a means of preparing men for conversion. Yet, he recognized that not everyone who enjoyed the Gospel was converted by it. He said the same about the works of creation, the law

76. Stoddard, *Galatians 3:1*, 134, 140, 143.

77. Perry Miller claims that Stoddard brought the Puritan founders' distinction between outward and inward covenants to its inevitable conclusion. He says that Stoddard "wanted to solve the intolerable dilemma of the sacraments. The covenant which God makes with a visible people is visible, and does not require sanctifying grace; hence the people have a 'natural power' to attend the visible ordinances. Unregenerate men are not in the internal covenant, yet they may be in the external. . . . Churches therefore judge only of appearances, not of realities. . . . To stand upon the ancient (and mistaken) doctrine of New England, that men are commanded to come but damned if they come unworthily, is, said Stoddard, 'unreasonable.'" Miller, *Mind*, 277.

or covenant of works, and the works of providence.[78] They were all a means of preparing men for conversion, but they did not convert; only the grace of God did that and He is under no obligation to do so. "God is not bound to change your heart. God is absolutely free. He may help you but, if He will not, He is blessed forever. . . . He may help you . . . but that lays Him under no necessity. It is His choice whether He will glorify His justice or mercy."[79]

Solomon Stoddard's solution for the spiritual decline of New England was not to follow the pattern of the Puritan Founders and tighten the restrictions of membership so as to purify the Church. On the contrary, it was to throw open the doors of the church to all professing believers so that they might worship God, who is worthy to be worshipped by regenerate and unregenerate alike. To Stoddard, if the church was like an army of worshippers, then opening Communion to all members was like the draft,[80] exposing more recruits to the converting grace of God. And though God is sovereign, "there is an infinite ocean of mercy in the heart of God . . . that God has provided a glorious way of salvation through Christ so that all who believe in Him shall be saved."[81]

"Evangelism was the heart and soul of Stoddard's ministry. His views on church polity and the terms of communion caused much more stir in his own day; but it was his books on conversion, his evangelistic sermons, and his example of a soul-winner that were in the long run most powerfully to influence American religion."[82]

---

78. Stoddard, "The Gospel is the Means of Conversion," 26–28.

79. Stoddard, "Preach the Gospel to the Poor," 96.

80. Walsh, 107.

81. Stoddard, Guide, 1.

82. Schafer, Theology of Revival, 335.

# 5

## The Influence of Solomon Stoddard

> Mr. Stoddard's principle at first made a great noise in the coun-
> try; and he was opposed, as introducing something contrary to
> the principles and practice of almost all the churches in New
> England, and the matter was publicly controverted between him
> and Dr. Increase Mather. However, through Mr. Stoddard's great
> influence over the people of Northampton, it was introduced
> there, though not without opposition: by degrees it spread among
> ministers and the people in that county, and in other parts of
> New England. At the settlement of Mr. Edwards, in 1727, this
> alteration in the qualifications required for admission into the
> church had been in operation about twenty-two or three years;
> a period during which the great body of the members of any
> church will be changed. This lax plan of admission has nowhere
> been adopted by a church, for any considerable length of time,
> without introducing a large proportion of members who are des-
> titute of piety; and although Mr. Stoddard was in other respects
> so faithful a minister, and so truly desirous of the conversion and
> salvation of his people, there can be no doubt, that such must
> have been the result during so long a period in the church of
> Northampton.[1]

THERE IS LITTLE QUESTION that Solomon Stoddard was influential.
Although Edwards' *Memoirs* cast Stoddardism in a negative light, they
do affirm that Stoddard himself wielded great influence over the church
of Northampton and the churches of the Connecticut Valley. However,
today, Stoddard's influence and contribution to the evangelical church
and the history of revival is not fully appreciated because most of what

---

1. Edwards, "Memoirs," cxv.

we know about Stoddard has come to us as a kind of marginal note by Edwards' scholars.[2]

How influential was Stoddard in Northampton? Historians do not agree. James Goulding claims that "Stoddard faced little opposition from the church when he introduced his innovations."[3] Perry Miller calls Stoddard an "autocrat" who dominated the churches and forced his will upon them.[4] On the other hand, Paul Lucas is foremost among recent scholars who question Stoddard's dominant influence.

> Stoddard quickly learned about the "power of the fraternity" and the zeal of Northampton's reform-minded brethren. The narrative of conversion experience survived two decades of ministerial education. The rationale for open communion, the converting ordinance, fared worse. At the same 1690 meeting where the brethren abolished the narrative, Stoddard preached a sermon from Galatians 3:1, "that the Lord's Supper was a converting ordinance." He then asked for a vote and lost by the narrowest of margins. Younger members, reflecting the persuasiveness of Stoddard's personality, voted with him but the older members, including the ruling elder, voted against him. He continued his crusade for ratification for some years after but never came close to victory.[5]

In spite of the fact that disagreement exists as to how deep and wide the acceptance of his ideas ran within his church and throughout New England, there can be no question that the influence of the man Stoddard was indeed great. His intellect and education, his "blue collar" appeal, and the sheer dominance of his personality cannot be denied.

> A large amount of Stoddard's unparalleled influence, it seems, emerged from his unique charisma and alluring personality. As a stern yet sensitive man, Stoddard, according to his son-in-law, William Williams, always appeared "comely and grave," com-

2. However, Patricia Tracy and George Marsden, in their recent works on Jonathan Edwards, focus their first chapters on his background, emphasizing primarily the role that Solomon Stoddard played. See Tracy, *Jonathan Edwards*, introduction and chapter 1 and Marsden, *Jonathan Edwards*, introduction, chapter I and II.

3. Goulding, "The Controversy Between Solomon Stoddard and the Mathers," 339.

4. Perry Miller formed this conclusion based upon his study of comments made by descendents as well as the texts of many eulogies that followed Stoddard's death. Miller, *Mind*, 228–230.

5. Lucas, *Valley*, 157. It should be noted that Lucas drew the information for the last sentence of this quote from Edward Taylor's Notebook, entry dated "1690."

manding "reverence from all that saw him." Williams acknowledged furthermore that "his conversation was also grave, but
delightful and very profitable, accompanied with a very sweet af-
fability and a freedom from moroseness." The Northampton cler-
gyman also possessed a "quickness of apprehension, strength of
memory, together with a clear and solid judgment." His personal
abilities and charisma enabled the longtime minister to influence
his congregation and all those with whom he came in contact.
The people in his Northampton congregation, Jonathan Edwards
later affirmed, had such a "high veneration for him," that they
eventually began to "imitate" his mannerisms. Northampton's
ordinary churchgoers as well as its rulers, Edwards further acknowledged, considered it a great compliment to "be like him."
Stoddard's physical traits suited him well for life on the frontier
and enabled him to connect with the type of people who lived
and toiled alongside him. Stoddard's desire and ability to work
alongside his parishioners must have given the frontier minister
a "man-of-the-people" type of reputation.[6]

Stoddard's pulpit ability was second to none. He was a large man
who loomed over his congregation, maintaining eye contact with them
because he did not believe that a preacher should use notes.[7] A Bostonian
named Joseph Nash once described Stoddard in the following verse:

> His Venerable Looks let us descry
> He taller was than Mean or common size,
> Of lovely Look, with majesty in's Eyes.
> From Nature's Gate, he walked like King's on Earth
> There's scarce such Presence seen 'mongst humane breath.[8]

Harry Stout maintains that if anything separated Stoddard's
preaching from others in his day "besides raw talent, it was the single-
mindedness with which he pursued the New Birth. He sounded more
like first-generation ministers in England whose regular sermons were
simple and direct in language, homely in metaphor, and taken up with
the joys of supernatural conversion."[9] Stout goes on to say that Stoddard's
sermon themes brought a balance between fear and hope; the horrors of
hell were always followed by a call to hope in Christ. "Thus channeled

6. Christensen, 106-107.
7. Marsden, 119.
8. Miller, "Stoddard," 282.
9. Stout, 100.

between the emotions of misery and hope, Stoddard pressed his hearers for an immediate personal commitment. His was less a gradualist message centered on life-long covenant duties and proper obedience (though these were not ignored) than an invitation to emotional catharsis, intended to drive sinners to their knees, then raise them up to new life in Christ."[10]

Patricia Tracy goes so far as to describe Stoddard's powerful revival preaching as "psychological manipulation" that often traumatized his listeners.[11] Manipulation or not, Stoddard's Northampton revivals became so successful that Benjamin Coleman of Boston said "people ask what they must do to be saved."[12]

Stoddard was so passionate in the pulpit that even after Edwards came as his assistant, he continued to preach at least half of the Sundays in the month up until his death at eighty-six. Together with his grandson, he presided over one last "harvest" of souls where "he was permitted to witness a work of divine grace among some of his people; in the course of which about twenty were believed to be savingly converted."[13]

Another component of Stoddard's influence in Northampton was the presence and greatness of his son, John, born February 18, 1682.[14] John Stoddard did not choose the ministry like others in his family, but became a businessman, politician, and military leader. He rose to the rank of colonel in the militia; by 1710 became mayor of Northampton, and between 1716 and 1748 served as judge and member of the General Court.[15] He also served as a selectman and moderator of the town council. He was a justice of the peace and an expert in Indian affairs. Suffice it to say, the most significant lay person in Western Massachusetts was none other than Stoddard's own son.[16]

---

10. Ibid.

11. Tracy, *Jonathan Edwards,* 31.

12. Ibid., 19.

13. Edwards, "Memoirs," xxxviii.

14. *The Northampton Church Records,* (unclear page number) provides a list of Esther and Solomon Stoddard's children. Although Esther had three children from her previous marriage to Eleazer Mather, she bore eleven more with Stoddard. John was her seventh with her second husband. See also *Judd Manuscripts,* 499–502.

15. Tracy, 149–150.

16. Ibid., 47.

If Solomon Stoddard's influence benefited from his son's illus-
trious rise through the secular ranks, then it grew even greater
when John became his father's strongest ecclesiastical ally as well.
Given that John "inherited his father's idea that one should not
be too niggardly in extending baptism and church membership
to those who were a little unorthodox but sincere in their beliefs,"
they formed an effective team of likeminded rulers. Although
not in the ministry, John Stoddard possessed such "a great degree
of understanding in things belonging to Christianity," Edwards
later acknowledged, "that I scarce knew [a] divine whom I ever
found more able to enlighten the mind in cases of conscience."
With a distinguished secular and ecclesiastical leader at his
side, Solomon Stoddard presided over almost every aspect of
Northampton society.[17]

Although less well-known than John, Solomon Stoddard's son-in-
law, Joseph Hawley, who married his tenth child, Rebecca, also proved
to be an avid supporter and ally. "A deacon in Stoddard's Northampton
Church, Hawley provided much-needed support for his father-in-
law's various innovations, just as his son John provided Stoddard
with an important secular ally."[18] However, there is a sad footnote to
Hawley's life. On June 1, 1735, he committed suicide just as the revival
in Northampton was coming to a close under his nephew, Jonathan
Edwards. "Hawley . . . suffered from depression, which intensified his
turmoil in the throes of the revival."[19]

And then there was Solomon Stoddard's influential grandson,
Jonathan Edwards. Edwards often spoke with great respect and affection for his grandfather, and although he came to strongly disagree
with Stoddardism, he never spoke disparagingly of Stoddard or of his
influence.

> That venerable man, then in his 84th year [when Edwards was
> called to be his colleague and successor], had been minister
> of Northampton 55 years; and by his piety, his great energy of
> character, and his knowledge of mankind, had early acquired,
> and maintained through a long life, a singular degree of weight
> among the ministers and churches of New England. Though a
> close student, and an able and faithful preacher, he was in char-

17. Christensen, 117.
18. Ibid., 118.
19. Sweeney, *Jonathan Edwards and the Ministry of the Word*, 122.

acter a man of business, and of action; and, in all the important
ecclesiastical bodies of Massachusetts, he had for many years an
influence, which usually was not contested, and was almost always paramount. . . . While the existing members of the church,
with scarcely an exception, regarded him as their spiritual father,
all the acting inhabitants of the town had grown up under his
ministry, and had been accustomed, from infancy, to pay respect
to his person and character, and in deference to his opinions,
such as children pay to those of a loved and venerated parent.[20]

Stoddard was not only a riveting revival preacher to his own
Northampton, but also a favorite annual commencement speaker at
Harvard as well as at special gatherings of the General Court in Boston.
He was so popular that people would come "expecting and glad to
hear from him."[21] In fact, a special road was constructed between
Northampton and Boston to help facilitate his travel.[22]

As has already been mentioned, it was Stoddard who first got news
of the impending Indian conspiracy known as King Phillip's War of
1675 and he sent warnings to Boston which went unheeded. When the
magistrates wanted to abandoned the Connecticut Valley because of the
Indian threat, it was Stoddard who protested. In 1703 Stoddard wrote
to Governor Dudley suggesting that big dogs should be used to track
and hunt down Indians. This was just after Indians had first raided the
Deerfield Settlement where his son-in-law John Williams was the pastor
and married to Stoddard's step-daughter Eunice, who was killed in a
subsequent Indian raid.[23]

Stoddard was not a prolific author. However, he did publish a
number of books and sermons; among them were two books which
arguably were the finest works written in the generation just prior to
the eighteenth century.[24] The first book was *The Safety of Appearing at
the Day of Judgment in the Righteousness of Christ: Opened and Applied.*
It was first published in 1687, and Increase Mather refused to write a
commendation for it because he was still at odds with Stoddard over
the latter's view of broad membership. Perry Miller describes this work

20. Edwards, "Memoirs," xxxvii.

21. Trumbull, 62–63.

22. Miller, *Stoddard*, 279.

23. Ibid., 280–281.

24. A valuable bibliographic synopsis of all Stoddard's writing can be found in
Coffman, 215–216.

as one of the top books in "American intellectual history."[25] Thomas
Schafer notes that this was Stoddard's finest work on conversion and it
was reprinted in 1729 at his death, and again in 1742 at the height of the
Great Awakening.[26] It was also reprinted in 1804, and John Erskine of
Edinburgh wrote the foreward which bears witness to Stoddard's influ-
ence at home and abroad:

> Mr. Stoddard was pastor about 60 years of a church at
> Northampton, New England, where he died in 1729, in the 86th
> year of his age. His sermons were searching and experimental,
> yet rational and argumentative; and often peculiarly suited for
> awakening the secure, directing the great work of Salvation, and
> afflicting the doubtful in judging their spiritual state. Thrice in
> the course of his ministry, there were remarkable seasons of gen-
> eral religious concern, and of numerous conversions among his
> people. It is no wonder then that one so diligent and successful
> in the work of the Lord, was highly esteemed and beloved by a
> church, most of whose members had been brought up under
> his ministry. Though his station was in a remote corner of New
> England, his strength of genius, depth of judgment, acuteness in
> reasoning, and knowledge of divinity, were so uncommon, that
> in difficult cases, his advice was much sought and valued, and his
> influence great throughout the whole of that country.[27]

Stoddard's second significant work was *A Guide to Christ* and was
published in 1714 just as Jonathan Edwards' generation was entering
ministerial training. It was reprinted in 1735 during the Northampton
revival. Stoddard once again asked Increase Mather to write the foreward to the book. By this time, their controversy had cooled and Mather
graciously consented. The last paragraph of this foreword is a touching
tribute to the deep respect these two old warriors had for each other:
"It is known that in some circles (not fundamentals in religion) I dif-
fer from this beloved author. Nevertheless, as there was a difference of
opinion between Jerome and Austin, Jerome said for all that, 'I cannot
but love Christ in Austin.' So do I say concerning my brother Stoddard.
And I pray the Lord to bless this, and all his holy labors for the conversion and salvation of many of God's elect."[28]

25. Ibid., 285.
26. Schafer, *Theology of Revival*, 333.
27. Stoddard, *Safety*, 2.
28. Stoddard, *Guide*, xiv.

Since there is little doubt regarding Stoddard's influence, what about the influence of Stoddardism in Northampton? We know that the church in Northampton was more aligned to the latitudinarian developments in Connecticut than with the strict Congregationalism of Boston and of its first pastor, Eleazer Mather. The church knew that its new pastor (Stoddard) would implement the provisions of the Half-Way Covenant. On November 5, 1672, just one month after Stoddard was ordained, the church all but eliminated the "state of education" and allowed all baptized adults who were morally above reproach to enter the church as full members without examining whether or not they were regenerate.[29] Then exactly five years later to the day, Stoddard simply stopped keeping church records, no longer delineating whether his parishioners were full or half-way members.[30]

> At one fell swoop he cured the evils of the Half-Way Covenant by going beyond it; he uprooted the New England Way in Northampton, and identified the visible church no longer with the communion of the saints, but with the town meeting—where he himself was dictator and lawgiver. There is evidence that he did not at first carry all the people with him, and great as was his authority, their turbulence was such that for a time he "knew not what to do with them. . . . The heat of spirit was raised to such a degree, that it came to hard blows," but "Pope" Stoddard forced his will upon them, and in his last years they were with him to a man.[31]

However, contrary to Perry Miller's assessment of this 1677 event, there is little evidence to substantiate its significance. There is nothing but silence on the matter in the church records. In fact, it was not until 1688 that there was any indication that the practice of open Communion had been implemented.[32] Edwards confirmed this by saying that open membership had been "established in Northampton without so much as one opposer to it."[33] Thus, contrary to Miller and Lucas, we have no

29. Lucas, *Valley*, 137.

30. Coffman, 43.

31. Miller, *Stoddard*, 298.

32. Edward Taylor's 1688 comments on this innovation indicate that it had been recently implemented in Northampton with little debate. See Davis, *Taylor versus Stoddard*, 10.

33. Christensen, 123.

indication that "Pope" Stoddard forced his will on the issue in 1688 or that the debate on the subject turned rancorous.

The next step in the development of Stoddardism in Northampton was hallmarked by the sermon he preached on Gal 3:1 on October 5, 1690. It was at this time he clearly articulated his view on the Lord's Supper as a converting ordinance. This was not a new development to Stoddard, even though it stirred the ire of both Mather and Taylor in a new way. Stoddard had for years consistently "maintained that the Lord's Supper was a converting ordinance in a way that all other church ordinances were."[34] For example, he did so in his 1687 work *The Safety of Appearing.*

Once again, there is no evidence that Stoddard forced the issue of getting the church to adopt this perspective on the Lord's Supper. In fact, it was not until 1704 that we have record of this becoming the official position of the church. Edwards mentioned this date in two places in his *Memoirs.* The following quote describes the history of the ministry at Northampton that Edwards inherited. The second quote describes the reasons for the difficulties he had in his ministry at Northampton.

> One circumstance, relating to the actual condition of the church at Northampton, deserves to be mentioned here, as it had an ultimate bearing on some of the most important events recorded in these pages. That church, like the other early churches of New England, according to the original platform, admitted none to the sacrament of the Lord's Supper, except those who, after due examination, were regarded in the judgment of Christian charity as regenerate persons. Such was the uniform practice of the church, from the time of its formation, during the life of Mr. Mather, and for upwards of thirty years after the settlement of Mr. Stoddard. How early Mr. Stoddard changed his own views on this subject, cannot be ascertained; but he attempted, in 1704, and, though not without opposition, yet with ultimate success, to introduce a corresponding change in the practice of the church. Though no vote was taken to alter the rules of admission, yet the point of practice was yielded. The Sacrament, from that time, was viewed as a converting ordinance, and those who were not regarded, either by themselves or others, as possessed of piety, were encouraged to unite themselves to the church.[35]

34. Walsh, "Open Communion," 111.
35. Edwards, "Memoirs," xxxvii–xxxviii.

Mr. Stoddard publicly avowed a change in his opinion in 1704, when he had been in the ministry at Northampton *thirty-two years*, and endeavored at that time to introduce a corresponding change in the practice of the church. He then declared himself, in the language of Dr. Hopkins, to be "of the opinion, that un-converted persons, considered as such, had a right in the sight of God, or by his appointment, to the sacrament of the Lord's Supper; and that thereby it was their duty to come to that ordi-nance, though they knew they had no true goodness or evan-gelical holiness." He maintained that visible Christianity does not consist in profession, or appearance of that wherein true holi-ness, or real Christianity, consists; that therefore the profession, which persons make, in order to be received as visible members of Christ's church, ought not to be such as to express or imply a real compliance with, or consent to, the terms of this covenant of grace, or a hearty embracing of the gospel: so that they who re-ally reject Jesus Christ, and dislike the gospel way of salvation in their hearts, and know that this is true of themselves, may make a profession without lying and hypocrisy.[36]

A first observation on these quotes is that while the Northampton church may have held to a strict requirement for admission to the Lord's Supper, the church was not uniformly agreed on it "from its formation during the ministry of Mr. Mather, and for a considerable period after the settlement of Mr. Stoddard" (as quoted above). On the contrary, from its inception, Northampton leaned toward the Half-Way Covenant and opposed the stricter methods of Eleazar Mather. As has already been mentioned, it took only one month after Stoddard's ordination to basi-cally eliminate the "state of education" and to allow all baptized adults who were morally above reproach to enter into full membership of the church; and just sixteen years until open admission to the Lord's Supper was instituted (1688). "The adoption of the 1672 reform explained par-tially why a majority of the church eventually agreed to end the relation of experience. Obviously if the children of the church gained member-ship on the basis of past conduct and an expressed willingness to abide by the terms of the covenant, few persons seeking full membership faced the prospect of a narrative of conversion experience. In Northampton, as in many towns, the narrative simply became excess baggage."[37]

36. Ibid., cxv.
37. Lucas, *Valley*, 137.

Another observation on the *Memoirs* takes issue with the implication that in 1704 the dam of Stoddardism broke and all that Stoddard had secretly kept to himself flooded the church and was made public. (Perhaps Edwards was speaking more from his own experience of keeping his misgivings about Stoddardism secret for so long.)[38] On the contrary, there seems to be more evidence for gradualism. Since no one seemed to know when Stoddard "changed his own views on the subject," it lends support to the idea that he did not force his views upon the church. Instead, it would seem more accurate to say that the church changed organically, partially because it was headed that way from the beginning and partially in response to his guidance and teaching.[39]

A third observation is that these paragraphs in Edwards' "Memoirs" contain some misrepresentations of Stoddard's view. The first quoted paragraph tells us that "those who were not regarded, either by themselves or others, as possessed of piety, were encouraged to unite to the church." This does not take into consideration Stoddard's basic premise that the covenant was open to all visible saints who professed faith in Jesus Christ and did not live a scandalous life. Stoddard believed that no human could tell who was a real (invisible) saint; only the free will of God determined that. And since no one was able to tell who was truly redeemed, the invitation was made that all should come and "feel safe" before God because they were invited to come according to God's Word.[40] Stoddard's main concern was not to preserve a pure church but to convert sinners to Christ, and his entire ecclesiology flowed from this.[41]

In the second quoted paragraph from the *Memoirs*, there are shades of Edwards' criticism of Stoddard's view found in *Humble Inquiry*. Edwards went to great pains to compare and define the concepts of *real* and *unreal*; *visible* and *invisible*. Edwards indicted Stoddard with encouraging those "who really reject Jesus Christ, and dislike the gospel way of salvation in their hearts, and know that this is true of themselves" to make a profession of faith without being called liars and hypocrites.

---

38. Edwards, "Humble Inquiry," 432.

39. Lucas, *Valley*, 136. Lucas claims that the 1672 reform continued until 1714, when the church agreed to baptize all "professing Christians" and their offspring and place them under church watch.

40. Stoddard, *Safety*, 39.

41. Jones, *Shattered Synthesis*,113.

"To say a man is a visible saint, but not visibly a real saint, but only visibly a visible saint is an absurd way of speaking; it is as much as to say, he is to appearance an appearing saint, which is in effect to say nothing."[42]

Stoddard was no longer around to defend his views, and Edwards' criticism was based upon his perception of the impact of those views during his two-decade pastorate at Northampton. What was never mentioned was the original context for Stoddard's emphasis on "visibility" in the face of a spiritual environment of nominalism and hypocrisy. Against the background of the Half-Way Covenant, Stoddard knew that the external covenant of the church had been separated from the internal Covenant of Grace. Thus instead of patching them together to preserve the New England Way, he claimed that "the covenant which God makes with a 'visible' people has nothing to do with the covenant of salvation; it binds merely to external observance."[43] The church, therefore, "is to act upon that which is visible."[44] To go beyond the visible was to enter a sphere known only by God. "Visible Saintship and Real Saintship, may consist with a great deal of iniquity in the Conversation for a time."[45]

Once again, Stoddard believed that there were no infallible signs of regeneration and no biblical rules for distinguishing saints and hypocrites.[46] The elect often do not evidence their election by how they live. Even Increase Mather recognized that hypocrites had slipped into the church and that the saints should be content with a "probable hope" rather than an absolute assurance of their salvation.[47] Therefore, Stoddard defined the visible saint as one who professed faith in Christ, who could say "yes" to the creeds.[48] Perry Miller claims that this is where Stoddardism was an ingenious solution to the problems caused by the Half-Way Covenant.

> On this argument Stoddard worked out one of his most ingenious conclusions, that since visible Christianity does not consist in true faith, the act of "owning" the covenant does not imply a real compliance with the Gospel and can be performed by those

42. Edwards, *Inquiry*, 437.
43. Miller, *Stoddard*, 303.
44. Stoddard, *An Appeal to the Learned*, 73.
45. Stoddard, *The Doctrine of Instituted Churches*, 6.
46. Miller, *Mind*, 283.
47. Ibid., 307.
48. Ibid.

who really in their hearts reject Christ! "When such profess faith, they make a true Profession, they profess that which they do indeed believe, though their profession be not graciously sincere, & men are bound to speak the truth, though they only do it with a moral, and not with a gracious sincerity." (*An Appeal to the Learned*, 9.) Such men should not be debarred from the sacrament, and they who do not know enough about the creed to qualify as visible Christians "may soon be sufficiently informed." (*Doctrine of Instituted Churches*, 19.) "It is unreasonable to believe Men to be visible Saints from their Infancy till they be forty or fifty years of Age, and yet not capable of coming to the Lords Supper, for want of the Exercise of Faith." (*Doctrine of Instituted Churches*, 20.) It is much better, and also more in accord with Biblical example, to baptise all who will be baptised, and send them as soon as possible to the Supper in the hope they may get some good from it.[49]

The language that Stoddard used opened him up to the criticism that he allowed known hypocrites or those who knowingly rejected Christ to come to the Lord's Table, but that was far from his intent. Anyone who professed faith in Christ and who had a "moral sincerity" (honesty of profession), even though it was not a "gracious sincerity" (profession of godliness), should not be prevented from receiving the Lord's Supper.[50]

Therefore, even if the communicant was "in reality" unregenerate (or at least did not know if he was regenerate), his honest and sincere profession qualified him for the Table. The Lord's Supper then was not just for the strengthening of the Saints, but a means also to work saving regeneration.[51] "All other Ordinances are appointed for Regeneration: Prayer, hearing the Word, Baptism; so likewise the censures [disciplines] are, that the Soul may be saved in the Day of the Lord Jesus; they are to further Mens Regeneration, in case they be not Converted already, and it would be strange if the Lords Supper alone should not be appointed to that end, whereas it hath a proper tendency thereunto, and many that come to that Ordinance by the appointment of Christ stand in as much need of it, as those that partake of other Ordinances."[52] Thus Stoddard

49. Miller, *Stoddard*, 307.
50. Stoddard, *Appeal to the Learned*, 9.
51. Stoddard, *Instituted Churches*, 22.
52. Ibid.

believed that he was remedying the spiritual compromise and "the tormenting dilemma of the Lord's Supper" that had been caused by the Half-Way Covenant.[53]

In the same way, Edwards believed that he needed to remedy the spiritual deadness and nominalism that he felt had been caused by Stoddardism. By the late 1740's Edwards clarified his view on the Sacraments and believed them to be signs and seals of saving grace. He did not go all the way back to Cotton's Code of only a regenerate membership or the Brownist notion of the pure church. He knew that even the purest church would be a mixture of wheat and tares and that no minister had the ability to ultimately discern the Elect. However, he did believe that a "profession of godliness" and not just a profession of faith was necessary to approach the Table.[54] In other words, the communicant should be "in the eye of a reasonable judgment . . . truly saints or godly persons and not just 'morally sincere.'"[55]

Ian Murray writes, "Similarly, Edwards says that a minister may have 'suspicions and fears' about a particular candidate for communion and yet have no sufficient ground to debar him from membership. Or again, an individual may have no assurance about his own salvation and yet be received, 'however he himself might scruple his own conversion' (*Works*, I, 488). Edwards denied as a falsehood that he 'insisted on persons being assured of their being in a state of salvation in order to my admitting them into the church' (*Works*, I, cxcviii)."[56]

The very influential Edwards lived under the shadow of Stoddard's influence throughout his ministry. In addition to other factors, Edwards' decision to depart from the policy of his grandfather on admission to the Lord's Supper was "strenuously opposed"[57] and though he was asked to write down his views in book form, he had already fallen into disfavor and his days in Northampton were numbered. His Uncle John Stoddard had passed away, thus removing his greatest shield of protection. In the preface to his *Humble Inquiry*, he tried to explain why he changed his mind about his grandfather's position twenty years after Stoddard's

---

53. Miller, *Stoddard*, 313.

54. Edwards, "Humble Inquiry," 487.

55. Ibid., 439. Also see Schafer, "Jonathan Edwards' Conception of the Church," 51–66.

56. Murray, *Jonathan Edwards: A New Biography*, 334.

57. Sweeney, *Edwards*, 142.

death. Even his explanation and ultimate dismissal from the church in Northampton demonstrated the kind of continuing influence Stoddard had on Edwards.

> I have formerly been of his opinion, which I imbibed from his books, even from my childhood, and in my proceedings conformed to his practice; though never without some difficulties in my view, which I could not solve. Yet, however, a distrust of my own understanding, and a deference to the authority of so venerable a man, the seeming strength of his arguments, together with the success he had in his ministry, and his great reputation and influence, prevailed for a long time to bear down my scruples. But the difficulties and uneasiness on my mind increasing, as I became more studied in divinity, and as I improved in experience; this brought me to closer diligence and care to search the Scriptures, and more impartially to examine and weigh the arguments of my grandfather, and such other authors as I could get on his side of the question. By which means, after long searching, pondering, viewing, and reviewing, I gained satisfaction, became fully settled in the opinion I now maintain.[58]

What was Stoddard's influence beyond Northampton—on the Connecticut Valley and the rest of Massachusetts? Once again there is a difference of opinion by scholars. Harry Stout asserts that "few ministers accepted Stoddard's iconoclastic innovations, but none denied his success in building Northampton into the largest, most influential church in the Connecticut River Valley."[59] Edward Taylor scholars Thomas and Virginia Davis claim that "the picture of Stoddard which emerges is not that of the veritable 'Pope' of the Connecticut Valley."[60] David Hall states that "few if any of the clergy appropriated the concept of the Lord's Supper as a converting ordinance."[61]

Paul Lucas agrees and calls the very notion that Stoddard was the "Pope" of the Connecticut Valley a myth.[62] He believes that this contention by Perry Miller was based upon "Increase Mather's suspicions and J. R. Trumbull's *History of Northampton.* Trumbull, while arguing that

---

58. Edwards, "Humble Inquiry," 432.

59. Stout, *New England Soul*, 99.

60. Davis, *Taylor vs. Stoddard*, 17.

61. Hall, *The Works of Jonathan Edwards*, 42.

62. It seems, however, that Lucas contradicts himself and elsewhere refers to Stoddard as the "Pope" of the Connecticut Valley. Lucas, "Solomon Stoddard," 742.

'Stoddardeanism' swept the Valley, offered no documentation, only the common assumption of other nineteenth-century chroniclers of Valley ecclesiastical history."[63] Instead Lucas believes Stoddard was a maverick who was revered by many and opposed by everyone. "Stoddard's influence, and it was considerable, stemmed from his personality, not from his theology or ecclesiology."[64]

In contrast, Ian Murray says that Stoddard's views "led to a temporary controversy in New England but soon became widely accepted in the churches and had been long established in Northampton by 1727."[65] George Marsden writes that "not only in Northampton but throughout the region, Stoddard was a force. Like a feudal baron whose power depended on personal allegiances, he used kinship ties to connect with other powerful clergy, merchants, and magistrates."[66] Miller claims that all the towns of the Valley had fallen in with Stoddard's views by 1700 except for Pelham, Belchertown, and Enfield.[67] James Jones says that Stoddard "brought most of the churches in Western Massachusetts and the Connecticut Valley along with him in his innovation."[68] Charles Randolph Coney, in his doctoral dissertation on the controversy between Edwards and the Northampton church, asserts that by 1708, the Connecticut Valley "was almost entirely under Stoddard's theological influence."[69] Williston Walker also had this to say about the influence of Stoddardism: "Though never adopted by a majority of New England churches, it (Stoddardism) was widespread in Western Massachusetts and Connecticut during the eighteenth century."[70]

The difficulty in assessing the influence of Stoddardism depends on whether it is narrowly or broadly defined. Jones defines it narrowly as allowing "all baptized persons full membership."[71] W.L. Kingsley also-

63. Lucas, *Appeal,* 258.

64. Ibid., 261.

65. Murray, 89.

66. Marsden, *Edwards,* 114.

67. Miller, "Solomon Stoddard," 303.

68. Jones, 107.

69. Coney, 61

70. Williston Walker, *Creeds and Platforms,* 280.

71. Ibid.

defines it narrowly as "the particular view respecting the admission of persons to the sacrament of the Lord's Supper."[72]

It is more appropriate to define it broadly, thereby appreciating more fully the variety of Stoddardism's appeal. There were three distinct elements to it: First, there was what has been defined by Lucas as a more Presbyterian element known as the "broad way" or "open Communion," as it was sometimes called.[73] It admitted into full membership with access to the Lord's Supper those who professed faith in Christ and lived a morally upright life.

Secondly, there was also the element of Stoddardism which held that the Lord's Supper was not only a sign and seal of salvation meant for the strengthening of the believer, but could be a converting ordinance for the visible saint who might still be unregenerate. Even Edwards himself preached a sermon in his early days on the Lord's Supper that sounded very much like his grandfather.[74]

Third, the last element in Stoddard's system was his view of the Instituted Church. He claimed that there was an "invisible church" composed of all the elect of God. He also believed that there was the "visible church" which included all visible saints and their children who professed faith in Jesus Christ. Stoddard also saw in the pages of the Old Testament a third kind of church; a church patterned after God's Covenant with the nation of Israel, which he called an "Instituted Church." "A[n Instituted] Church is a Society of Saints joined together, according to the appointment of Christ for the constant carrying on of his publick Worship."[75]

Stoddard believed that the Congregationalist principle of a particular church consisting of a gathering of saints bound together by a mutual covenant was nowhere pictured in the New Testament. He believed it to be too individualistic and independent.[76] "We never read of any particular Covenant made in the Synagogues, which Answer to our Congregations, whereby the Members of one Synagogue were bound

---

72. Kingsley, "Stoddardeanism," 350.

73. Lucas, *Valley,* 149.

74. Edwards, "The Spiritual Blessings of the Gospel Represented as a Feast," 290.

75. Stoddard, *Instituted,* 5.

76. Stoddard believed that if it were left up to the individual to covenant with a particular church, then it could very well be that such an individual would covenant with no church and therefore fail to engage in the public worship of God.

one to another."[77] If a Christian lived in a town where there was a church, that Christian should be bound to join it. If several churches were in the town, then human prudence should be used to divide the town accordingly. The purpose of the Instituted Church was for the public worship of God. And the elements of this worship were prayer, singing of Psalms, preaching and teaching, baptism, the Lord's Supper, church discipline, and the authoritative blessing of the people by the ministers in the Name of God.[78] "This [then] was the core of Stoddard's 'Presbyterianism.' His attacks on restrictive membership requirements, church covenants, and congregational government, and his advocacy of open communion, converting ordinances, synodical government, and national churches were tied together neatly in a package labeled the Instituted Church. Was the Instituted Church also the church of New England's Presbyterians? Was Stoddard their spokesman, or was he a maverick whose views were peculiarly his own?"[79]

It is evident that Stoddard did not speak for the Presbyterians[80] in the Connecticut Valley or anywhere else. When Increase Mather published his *Order of the Gospel* in 1700, Benjamin Coleman of the Brattle Street Church in Boston, Simon Bradstreet of Charlestown, and Timothy Woodbridge of Hartford replied in *Gospel Order Revived* (1700). Mather had attacked these three for their Presbyterian innovations and connected them with Stoddard's Instituted Church. Their reply, however, not only took issue with Mather on his interpretation of New England ecclesiastical history, but also dissociated themselves from Stoddard.[81]

Is there any evidence, then, that Stoddard's views were adopted anywhere in the Connecticut Valley outside Northampton? Lucas claims that the records of churches in the Connecticut Valley do not support the influence of Stoddardism apart from the influence of his person-

---

77. Ibid., 7.

78. Ibid., 15-24.

79. Lucas, "Appeal," 267.

80. "Many moderate Congregationalists appeared Presbyterian-like in their ecclesiastical views, so much so that before 1660 the term 'Presbyterian' was often used to deride the moderates. The epithet identified any cleric or layman who opposed a public or private narrative of conversion experience as a prerequisite for membership and favored admitting a person of high moral character who made a simple profession of faith." Lucas, *Valley*, 60.

81. Lucas, "Appeal," 272.

ality.[82] Lucas also claims that the concept of open Communion was a Presbyterian concept already held by a number of Connecticut churches.[83] As an example, he cites the First Church of Hartford which held to that position from 1660 to the death of Thomas Woodbridge in 1730. In Hartford it was known as "Mr. Woodbridge's Way" and had nothing to do with Stoddard or the concept of converting ordinance.[84]

Lucas further contends that there were only two Connecticut clergy who were connected to all of Stoddard's views: son-in-law Stephen Mix of Wethersfield and Gurdon Saltonstall of New London, who became governor in 1707.[85] However, some scholars would take issue with Lucas' assessment and add several more names to those of Mix and Saltonstall who became a part of Mr. Stoddard's Way. Philip F. Gura demonstrates that William Williams of Hatfield, another of Stoddard's sons-in-law, not only held to open Communion but also held to it as a converting ordinance. He quotes from a Williams sermon. "[There are] no precepts for, nor precedent of, insisting on . . . a profession of faith as the condition of admission to the Lord's Table. The matter of the worship of God in his ordinances is a step in the way that leads to repentance from sin, a step onward in the way to approach unto God . . . a step without the taking of which, a man can never worship God aright. [The Lord's Supper could lead to] the attainment of grace."[86]

In addition, Williams was one of the first ministers to sign on to the Hampshire Association[87] in 1714, the idea for which flowed out of Stoddard's Presbyterian treatise *The Instituted Church*. Williams seemed to have evidenced pure Stoddardism: open Communion, Communion as a converting ordinance, and involvement in an area ministerial council which was an important means of extending Stoddardism throughout the Connecticut Valley.[88]

82. Ibid., 277.

83. Ibid., 276. See also Pope, 251– 258.

84. Ibid.

85. Ibid., 274.

86. Gura, "Going Mr. Stoddard's Way," 491, 497.

87. See Appendix Document 7 for a 1715 two-page letter sent by the Hampshire Association to the Enfield Church (CT) which had censured its pastor (Nathaniel Collins) and denied him the right to serve Communion. The letter bears the signatures of the Association and may have been written by Stoddard himself— proof that his handwriting was legible on occasion.

88. Christensen makes the point that many of the sermons preached by the

A case could also be made for Stoddard's influence on another son-in-law, John Williams of Deerfield. Williston Walker lists the Deerfield church as "Stoddardean"[89] and Kevin Sweeney points out that John Williams was "part of a clerical network united by kinship and shared religious sentiments." He played a central part "in this growing party of related and like-minded Connecticut Valley ministers led by Stoddard, who stood at the lead."[90]

Stoddard's son, Anthony, was pastor of the Woodbury Church in Connecticut from 1702 to 1760. Anthony not only followed his father's example in terms of years spent in the ministry of one church, but also the example of his father's theology and ecclesiology. James Walsh provides evidence that Anthony was in line with Stoddardean principles and was in a position to extend that influence in his part of Connecticut.

> For one thing, it is likely that Woodbury practiced "Stoddardism"; that is, instead of demanding genuine signs of grace before allowing a person to receive the Lord's Supper, as Congregational theory generally required, it followed the ideas of Solomon Stoddard, who would admit to full church membership all baptized persons above the age of fourteen. Although there is no direct evidence that Woodbury was Stoddardean, Stoddard's son, Anthony, was pastor there from 1702 to 1760, and when a new pastor was ordained to succeed him, a new covenant was adopted which implicitly criticized the traditional practice of allowing persons to become communicants without subscribing to the covenant of grace. In addition, the Bethlehem [or Bethlem] First Church, which was an offshoot of the Woodbury church and probably inherited its practices, explicitly rejected unregenerate communion in 1750 after having followed it for ten years.[91]

Aaron Christensen in his doctoral dissertation makes a strong case for two more Stoddardean ministers in the Connecticut Valley: Isaac Chauncy of Hadley and Daniel Brewer of Springfield.[92] Williston Walker has already been mentioned regarding his list of Stoddardean and anti-Stoddardean churches based upon the 1750 council of ministers that met to arbitrate the dispute between Edwards and the Northampton

---

Hampshire clergy were outside their local churches. Christensen, 167.
  89. Walker, *Creed and Platforms*, 282.
  90. Sweeney, "River Gods," 152–153.
  91. Walsh, "Congregational Church of Woodbury," 545.
  92. Christensen, 170–176.

church.[93] Although the nine ministers that convened in Northampton on this occasion should have come from the twenty-five member Hampshire Association, two of the nine were from outside Hampshire County. Given that Edwards was allowed to choose five of the members that would form the core of the ecclesiastical council, historian W.L. Kingsley argues that two sympathetic outsiders were needed since "there were not more than three in the county, with the exception of his young brother-in-law, Moses Tuttle, that were decidedly anti-Stoddardean."[94] The other twenty-two members of the Hampshire Association, Kingsley and Walker both claim, were Stoddardean in their admission policies.

Kingsley further claims that at the time of Edwards' council, nearly all the churches in old Hampshire County, which at that time included present-day Hampshire, Hamden, Franklin, and Berkshire, embraced and practiced Stoddardean principles. "Stoddardeanism prevailed in this region for fifty years. A death blow was given to it by the controversy which grew out of the publication of Edwards' *Humble Inquiry*. It declined from the time of his [Edwards] dismission, until it was numbered with the opinions that had been." [95]

Finally, perhaps the best summary of the influence of Stoddardism has been given by Williston Walker. "These views of Stoddard spread widely and were adopted by many good men. The majority of the churches in Western Massachusetts accepted them, they were largely entertained in Connecticut, and the region about Boston was not without their representatives."[96]

93. "In 1750, at the time of Edwards' dismission from Northampton, the old Hampshire Association might be divided as follows: *Stoddardean*, Amherst, Brimfield, East Granville, Great Barrington, Greenwich, Hadley, South Hadley, Longmeadow, New Marborough, Northfield, Northampton, Sheffield, Shutesbury, Southampton, Springfield, West Springfield, Sunderland, Westfield, Wilbraham; Somers, Conn; Suffield, Conn.; *Anti-Stoddardean*, Belchertown, Enfield, Conn.; Pelham. Hatfield was doubtful. The following ministers defended Stoddardism at various times in print, George Beckwith, Lyme, Conn.; Charles Chauncy, First Church, Boston; Ebenezer Devotion, Scotland, Conn; Solomon Williams, Lebanon, Conn. These of course represent but a few of the real number of adherents." Walker, *Creed and Platforms*, 282.

94. Kingsley, 353.

95. Ibid.

96. Walker, *Creeds and Platforms*, 282.

# Afterword

...

STODDARD'S DEATH ON NOVEMBER 2, 1729, brought wide tribute from clergy all over New England. In Northampton, his son-in-law William Williams of Hatfield preached the funeral sermon from Zechariah 1:5, 6 entitled *The Death of a Prophet Lamented and Improved*. He ended his moving sermon with this tribute:

> You in this Place have particular reason to mourn; may take up the Prophets Lamentation, The Crown has fallen from our Heads! For how long a Time did GOD make him, the Light and Glory, the Strength and Beauty of this Place! Now proceeding in the Sixtieth year of his Ministry among you; and enabled profitably to continue in it, to the very Day he was seized with his last Sickness. Surely you can't forget how he has been with you at all seasons; in all Trials and Changes of Providence, you have pass'd under. And how he has instructed, warn'd, charg'd, and comforted you, as a Father his Children! With what constancy, cheerfulness, and unweariedness, he wore out his Life in your Service: how concerned to guide you to Christ, and to build you up in Faith and Holiness, to support and direct you in all your Fears and Temptations! How [fitted?] to speak a Word in Season to everyone that was weary! How great a Casuist! How accomplished a Divine! How truly excellent a Preacher! But while you lament your loss, you will remember from whence you had so great a Blessing; and I hope t'will excite and maintain among you a Spirit of Prayer for his Son and Successor; the Spirit of Elijah may rest on him: and that you will in all proper ways strengthen his Heart and Hands, under the weight of so much Work as is now rowl'd upon him.[1]

Benjamin Coleman, leader of the Brattle group, gave a memorial the following July at the Harvard commencement. "As a Peter here among the disciples . . . [he was] very much our primate and a prince among us, in an Evangelical and truly apostolical sense."[2]

1. Williams, *Death of a Prophet Lamented*, 28.
2. Coffman, 180.

Solomon Stoddard pushed Puritanism beyond the Half-Way Covenant, not for the purpose of liberalizing it, but for the purpose of converting the unconverted in any way possible. His "innovations" may have led to nominalism and even to further liberalizing, but the greatest problem with Stoddardism was the absence of Stoddard. After his death, his views were considered a deviation from traditional Protestant and Reformed thinking akin to the Papists and Arminians. He was also marginalized as being in the same camp as a minority of English Dissenters such as Humphrey, Timson, Blake, and Ward. Thomas Foxcroft wrote a letter to Jonathan Edwards (1749) and in it implied that Stoddard's views were so novel "that I wonder, (those of the contrary opinion) have not taken notice of it, there is an army to a man against them."[3]

However, when Stoddard was alive, his passion for evangelism and the glory of God formed a bit and bridle for his practices that kept them moving in a proper direction. He cannot be understood apart from his passion for the Gospel of Jesus Christ and for the salvation of souls.

In conclusion, this passion is revealed in a condensation of a sermon Stoddard preached on Luke 4:18, *To Preach the Gospel to the Poor*:

> You are wholly empty of goodness. . . . You have not power to do any good. . . . God is not bound to change your heart. God is absolutely free. He may help you but, if He will not, He is blessed forever. . . . It is not beyond His mercy to pardon you. . . . But as great as your sins are, it is not beyond the grace of God. . . . God has designed to save many lost sinners. . . . And He has done a great deal in order to the salvation of such sinners. The price of it is paid. Sin laid a bar in the way, but that bar is removed by the death of Christ. There is no need of any contrivance how to satisfy the law, that is done already by Christ. God has sent Christ to save us. . . . He tells you that you shall be welcome if you will come to Christ. . . . Yes, He beseeches you to come for salvation. God is of infinite majesty, yet He entreats you to be saved. He condescends to your infirmity and stoops so low as to plead with you. He becomes, as it were, a petitioner to you. He begs you to come, and urges it as a courtesy to come, with tenderheartedness He prays you to come. . . . This [then] is a principal way wherein God glorifies Himself. The end of all things is God's glory and . . . He glorifies Himself in working out the salvation of sinners by Christ.[4]

3. Foxcroft, "Being a Letter to the Author . . ." 339.
4. Stoddard, "To Preach the Gospel to the Poor."

# Appendix

Document 1: Article of "Gathering" in records of the First Church Northampton, April 18, 1661.

Document 2: On November 5, 1672, the church at Northampton basically eliminated the "state of education" for adults and took into full membership those who professed faith in Christ and were not scandalous in life.

Document 3: Solomon Stoddard's ordination on September 11, 1672, from the records of the First Church Northampton.

Document 4: A covenant used to admit younger persons into a type of half-way membership called "the state of education" dated November 5, 1672, from records of the First Church Northampton.

Document 5: A sample of Solomon Stoddard's microscopic handwriting; thanks to Forbes Library, Northampton MA.

Document 6: A one-line entry of Jonathan Edwards' dismissal from the First Church Northampton, June 22, 1750.

Document 7: A two-page letter (1715) sent by the Hampshire Association to the Enfield Church (CT), which had censured its pastor (Nathaniel Collins) and denied him the right to serve Communion. The letter bears the signatures of the Association and may have been written by Stoddard himself—indicating that his handwriting was legible on occasion.

Document 8: Signatures of those on the original church covenant in Northampton, April 18, 1661. Note the signatures of Eleazer and Esther Mather.

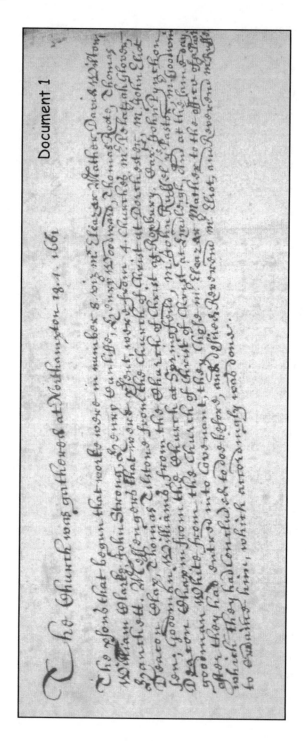

*Figure 2*

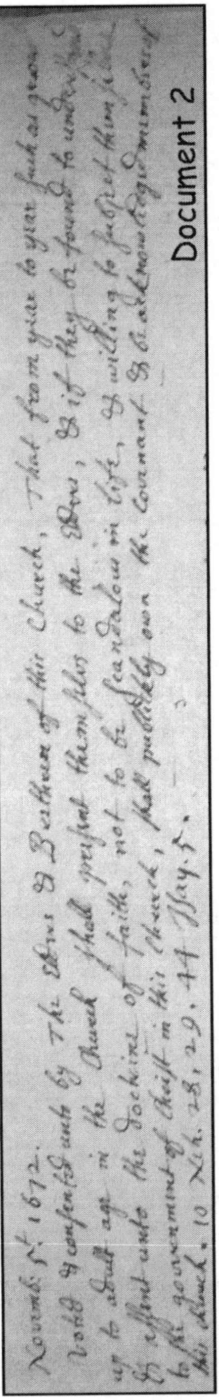

Document 2

November 8th 1672.

Voted & confessed unto by the Elders & Brethren of this Church, That from year to year such as grow up to Adult age in the Church shall present themselves to the Elders, & if they be found to understand & profess the Doctrine of faith, not to be Scandalous in life, & willing to subject themselves to the government of Christ in this Church, shall publickly own the Covenant & be admitted to full membership.

this Church. 10 Xi.b. 28, 29. 44 May. 5.

*Figure 3*

## Document 3

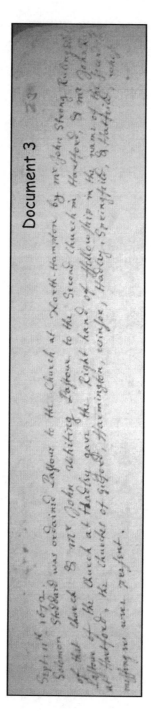

*Figure 4*

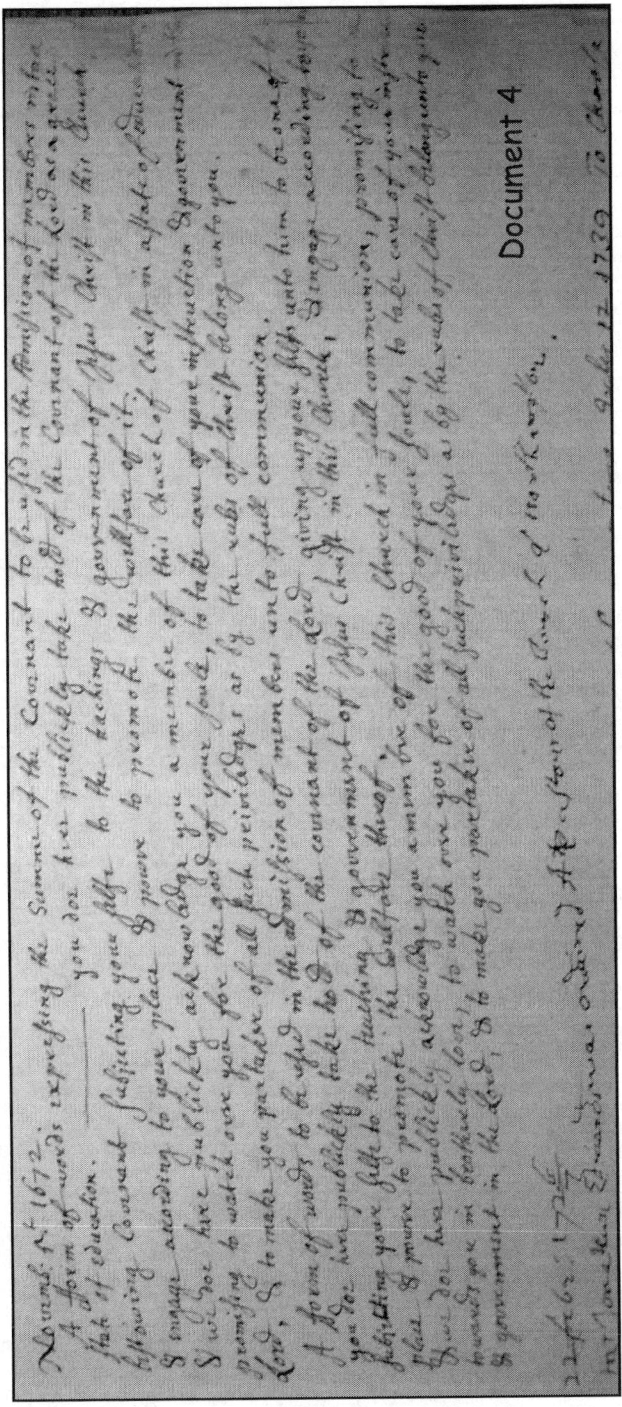

Novemb: 1st 1672.
A form of words expressing the Summe of the Covenant to be used in the Admission of members in a
state of education. ——— you doe here publickly take hold of the Covenant of the Lord as a grace
following Covenant subjecting your selfe to the teachings & government of Jesus Christ in this Church
& engage according to your place & power to promote the welfare of it,
& we doe here publickly acknowledge you a member of this Church of Christ in a state of education
promising to watch over you for the good of your soule, to take care of your instruction & government in the
Lord, & to make you partaker of all such priviledges as by the rules of Christ belong unto you.

A form of words to be used in the admission of members unto full communion.
you doe here publickly take hold of the covenant of the Lord, giving up your selfe unto him to be one of
subjecting your selfe to the teaching & government of Jesus Christ in this Church, & engage according to yo[ur]
place & power to promote the welfare thereof.
& we doe here publickly acknowledge you a member of this Church in full communion, promising to
towards you in brotherly love, to watch over you for the good of your soule, to take care of your instr[uction]
& government in the Lord, & to make you partaker of all such priviledges as by the rules of Christ belong unto you

Document 4

22 feb: 1726/7
Mr Jonathan Edwards was ordained A Pastour of the Church of Northampton.
... July 12 1730 To Charle...

*Figure 5*

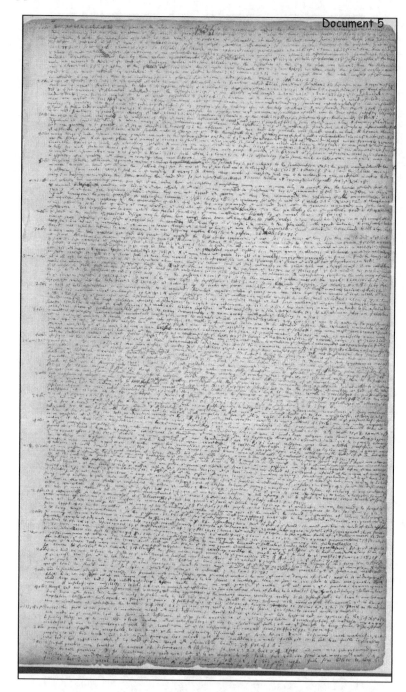

*Figure 6*

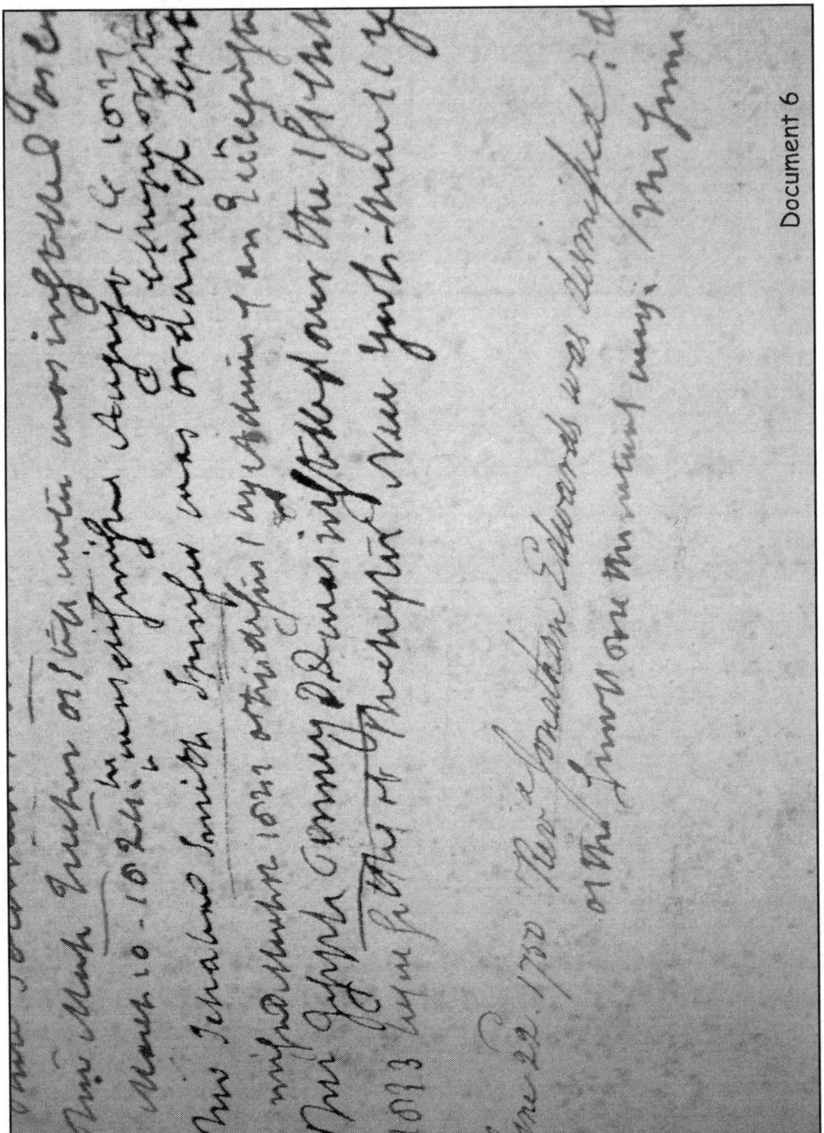

Document 6

*Figure 7*

Dear Brother                    # Document 7

We have been Informed from time to time & of late that
notwithstanding our indeavours to compose differences among
you, yet your divisions do continue, what did appear to be
just matter of offence was acknowledged, & we do not understand that mr Collins has given any occasion of greiff since
several persons belonging to other places, who have occasionally
heard him, abroad & at home, have given an Account
that his preaching hath been profitable & worthy to be accepted,
& some of your selves that remain unsatisfyed, have given
testimony that his preaching is minded, which makes us
quite at a loss how it comes about that your dissatisfactions
do continue.
It is the more exercising to us to hear of the continuance of
your discontents, because of the influence they have on mr
Collins to increase his bodily distemper, & so make his
work the more burdensome, the making of his work
heavy must needs be a damage to your selves as well as to him.
But we are especially puzled to conceive how you can
justify your selves in not allowing the Lords-Supper to be
administred, if he be fit to preach & baptize, surely he
is fit to administer the Lords-Supper, can you satisfy
your consciences to attend upon other parts of his ministry
for a twelvemonth together, yet not give way to his admi-
nistring the Lords-Supper, surely he has power from Christ
to dispence the ordinances of God, until he is in some
way of order suspended from the execution of his office,
you have not proved him scandalous, you have not proved
him insufficient, the word will be apt to judge two things
upon it, one is that you don't thirst after the ordinances
of God, the other is that you do it upon a disigne to affront
him & weary him out.
you sent for a Council the last year, what you had
to say was heard with patience, & a Determination
drawn up upon it, But you have acted since that
                                                as

Figure 8

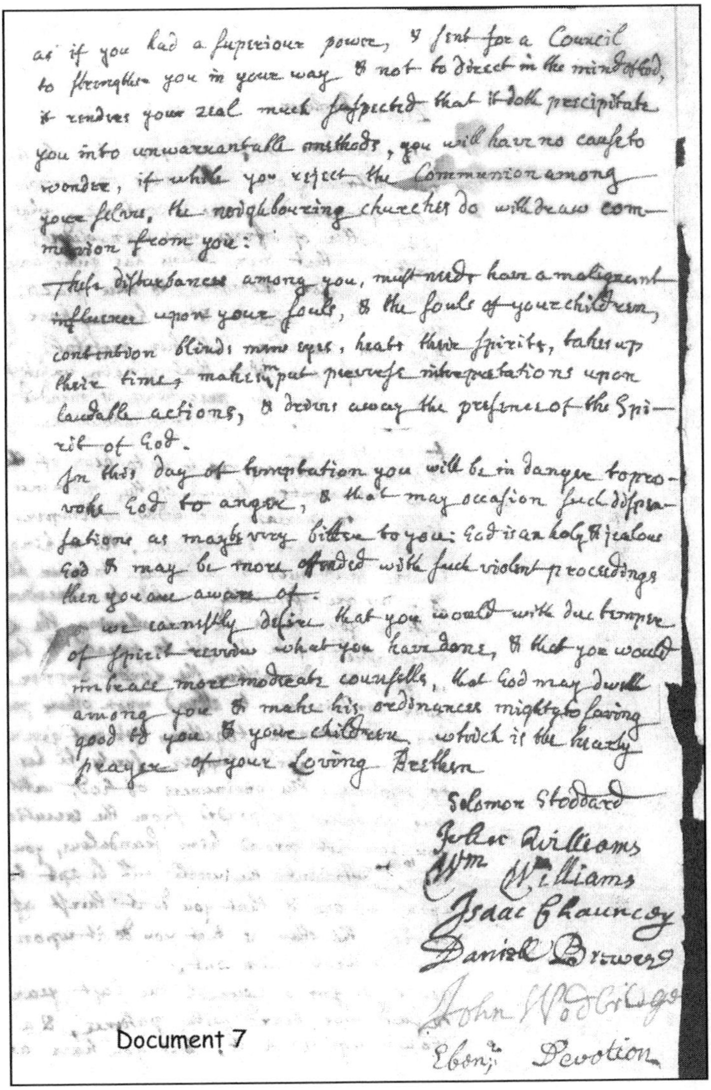

as if you had a superiour power, & sent for a Councill
to strengthen you in your way & not to direct in the mind of God,
it renders your zeal much suspected that it doth precipitate
you into unwarrantable methods, you will have no cause to
wonder, if while you reject the Communion among
your selves, the neighbouring churches do withdraw communion from you:

These disturbances among you, must needs have a malignant
influence upon your souls, & the souls of your children,
contention blinds mens eyes, heats their spirits, takes up
their time, makes them put peuvese interpretations upon
laudable actions, & drives away the presence of the Spirit of God.

In this day of temptation you will be in danger to pro-
voke God to anger, & that may occasion such dispra-
fations as may be very bitter to you: God is an holy & jealous
God & may be more offended with such violent proceedings
then you are aware of.

we earnestly desire that you would with due temper
of spirit review what you have done, & that you would
imbrace more moderate counsells, that God may dwell
among you & make his ordinances mighty to saving
good of you & youre children, which is the hearty
prayer of your Loving Brethren

Solomon Stoddard
John Williams
Wm Williams
Isaac Chauncey
Daniell Brewer
John Woodbridge
Ebenr Devotion

Document 7

*Figure 9*

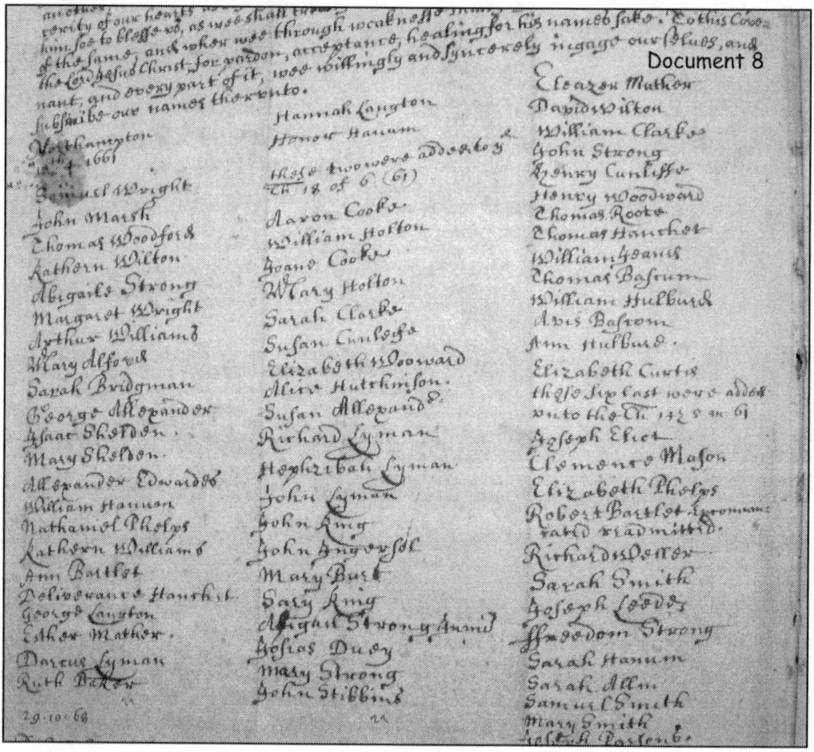

Figure 9

# Bibliography

Ahlstrom, Sydney. *A Religious History of the American People*. New Haven: Yale University Press, 1972.

Beasley-Murray, G. R. *Baptism in the New Testament*. Grand Rapids: Eerdmans Publishing Company, 1962.

Behnke, Michael. "Solomon Stoddard of Northampton." Honors thesis, Amherst College, 1966.

Boorman, David. "The Halfway Covenant." In *The Puritan Experiment*. London: The Westminster Conference, 1976.

Burg, B. R. "The Cambridge Platform: A Reassertion of Ecclesiastical Authority." *Church History* 43 (Dec 1974): 470–487.

Calvin, John. *Institutes of the Christian Religion*, 2 Vols, edited by J.T. McNeil and F. Lewis Battles. Philadelphia: Westminster John Knox Press, 1993.

Christensen, Aaron F. "Pope or Persuader: The Influence of Solomon Stoddard in Northampton and Western New England." PhD diss., Boise State University, 2005.

Clark, Samuel. *Antiquities, Historicals and Graduates of Northampton*. Steam Press of Gazette Print Co., 1882.

———. *Historical Catalogue of the Northampton First Church, 1661–1891*. Northampton, MA: Gazette Print Co., 1891.

Coffman, Ralph J. *Solomon Stoddard*. Boston: Twayne Publishers, 1978.

Coney, Charles Randolph. "Jonathan Edwards and the Northampton Church Controversy: A Crisis of Conscience." PhD diss., University of Texas at Arlington, 1989.

Cook, Paul E. G. "The Church." In *Anglican and Puritan Thinking*. London: The Westminster Conference, 1978.

Cooper, James F. *Tenacious of Their Liberties*. Oxford: Oxford University Press, 1999.

Cotton, John. *The Way of the Churches of Christ in New England*. London, 1643.

Davis, Thomas M., and Jeff Jeske. "Solomon Stoddard's 'Arguments' Concerning Admission to the Lord's Supper." *American Antiquarian Society* Vol. 86 (April 1976): 80.

Davis, Thomas M. and Virginia L. Davis. *Edward Taylor vs. Solomon Stoddard: The Nature of the Lord's Supper*. Boston: Twayne Publishers, 1981.

De Arteaga, William L. *Forgotten Power: The Significance of the Lord's Supper in Revival*. Grand Rapids: Zondervan, 2002.

De Jong, Peter Y. *The Covenant Idea in New England Theology, 1620-1847*. Grand Rapids: Eerdmans, 1945.

Edwards, Jonathan. "A Faithful Narrative of the Surprising Work of God." In *The Works of Jonathan Edwards*, Vol. 1, edited by Edward Hickman. Edinburgh: Banner of Truth, 1979.

———. "An Humble Inquiry into the Rules of the Word of God Concerning the Qualifications Requisite To A Complete Standing and Full Communion in the Visible Christian Church." In *The Works of Jonathan Edwards,* Vol. 1, edited by Edward Hickman. Edinburgh: Banner of Truth, 1979.

———. "Memoirs of Jonathan Edwards." In *The Works of Jonathan Edwards,* Vol. 1, edited by Edward Hickman. Edinburgh: Banner of Truth, 1974.

———. "The Spiritual Blessings of the Gospel Represented as a Feast." In *The Works of Jonathan Edwards,* Vol. 1, edited by Edward Hickman. Edinburgh: Banner of Truth, 1979.

Elton, G. R. *England under the Tudors.* London: Methuen, 1967.

Felt, Joseph B. *The Ecclesiastical History of New England.* Boston: 1855-1862.

Fleming, Sanford. *Children and Puritanism.* New York: Arno Press, 1969.

Foote, H. W., Ed. "The Significance of the Cambridge Platform of 1648." In *The Cambridge Platform of 1648: Tercentenary Commemoration.* Boston: Beacon, 1998.

Gildrie, Peter P. *The Profane, the Civil, and the Godly: The Reformation of Manners in Orthodox New England, 1679-1789.* University Park: Pennsylvania State University, 1994.

Gilsdorf, Joy. *The Puritan Apocalypse.* New York: Garland Publishing, 1989.

Goulding, James A. "The Controversy Between Solomon Stoddard and the Mathers: Western vs. Eastern Massachusetts Congregationalism." PhD diss., Claremont University, 1971.

Grabo, Norman S. "Edward Taylor on the Lord's Supper." *Boston Public Library Quarterly* Vol. 12 (January 1960): 22–85.

———. *Edward Taylor's Treatise Concerning the Lord's Supper.* Michigan State University Press, 1965.

Gura, Philip F. "Going Mr. Stoddard's Way: William Williams on Church Privileges." *William and Mary Quarterly* 45.3 (July 1988): 489–498.

Hall, David D., Ed. *The Works of Jonathan Edwards.* New Haven: Yale University, 1957–2003.

Haller, William. *The Rise of Puritanism.* New York: Harper & Row, 1938.

Hardman, Keith J. *The Spiritual Awakeners.* Chicago: Moody Press, 1983.

Haroutunian, Joseph. *Piety versus Moralism: The Passing of the New England Theology.* New York: Harper and Row, 1932.

Holifield, Brooks. "The Intellectual Sources for Stoddardism." *The New England Quarterly* 45, (Sept 1972): 373–392.

———. "The Renaissance of Sacramental Piety in Colonial New England." *William and Mary Quarterly* Vol. 29, (January 1972): 33–48.

Hooker, Thomas. *A Preparation to the Lords Supper, in the Paterne Exhibited in Gods Image in Adam.* London, 1640.

———. *A Survey of the Summe of Church-Discipline.* London, 1648.

Hutchinson, Thomas. *Collection of Papers Relating to the History of Massachusetts Bay.* Edited by Alden T. Vaughan. Hanover: University Press of New England, 1972.

Jamieson, John F. "Jonathan Edwards' Change of Position on Stoddardism." *Harvard Theological Review,* Vol. 74 (1981): 79–99.

Jones, James W. *The Shattered Synthesis.* New Haven: Yale University, 1973.

Kingsley, W. L. "Stoddardeanism." *The New Englander* Vol. IV (July 1846): 350–56.

Kling, David. *A Field of Divine Wonders.* University Park, PA: Pennsylvania State University Press, 1993.

Lepore, Jill. *The Name of War: King Philip's War and the Origins of American Identity.* New York: Alfred Knopf, 1998.

Lucas, Paul R. "An Appeal to the Learned: The Mind of Solomon Stoddard." William and Mary Quarterly Vol. 30, (April 1973): 257–292.

———. "Solomon Stoddard and the Origins of the Great Awakening." *The Historian* Vol. 59 (Summer 1997): 741–58.

———. *Valley of Discord: Church and Society along the Connecticut River, 1636–1725.* Hanover: The University Press of New England, 1976.

Marsden, George M. *Jonathan Edwards: A Life.* New Haven: Yale University, 2003.

Mather, Cotton. *A Companion for Communicants: Discourses Upon the Nature, the Design, and the Subject of the Lord's Supper; with Devout Methods of Preparing for, And Approaching to that Blessed Ordinance.* Boston: Samuel Green, 1690.

———. "Magnalia Christi Americana." In *Milestones of Thought in the History of Ideas*, Book III. Edited by Raymond Cunningham. New York: Frederick Ungar Publishing Company, 1970.

Mather, Increase. *A Discourse Concerning the Danger of Apostasy.* Boston, 1679.

Miller, Perry. *The New England Mind: From Colony to Province.* Cambridge: Harvard University Press, 1953.

———. *Orthodoxy in Massachusetts.* New York: Harper & Row, 1933.

———. "Solomon Stoddard: 1643-1729." *Harvard Theological Review* Vol. XXXIV (Oct 1941): 277–320.

Minkema, Kenneth. "The Edwardses: A Ministerial Family in Eighteenth-Century New England." PhD diss., University of Connecticut, 1988.

Morgan, Edmund S. *The Puritan Dilemma: The Story of John Winthrop,* 2nd Edition. New York: Longman, 1999.

———. *Visible Saints: The History of the Puritan Idea.* New York: New York University, 1963.

Murray, Ian H. *Jonathan Edwards: A New Biography.* Edinburgh: Banner of Truth, 1987.

New, John F. H. *Anglican and Puritan.* London: A. and C. Black, 1964.

Noll, Mark. *America's God: From Jonathan Edwards to Abraham Lincoln.* Oxford: Oxford University, 2002.

Parnham, David. "Redeeming Free Grace: Thomas Hooker and the Contested Language of Salvation." *Church History 4,* no. 77 (2008): 915–954.

Pope, Robert G. *The Half-Way Covenant: Church Membership in Puritan New England.* Princeton: Princeton University, 1969.

*Records of the First Congregational Church of Windsor Connecticut.* Connecticut State Library, Hartford, CT.

*Records of the First Congregational Church of Northampton.* Forbes Library, Northampton, MA.

Russell, John. "Collections." 4th ser., VIII. The Massachusetts Historical Society, Boston.

Schafer, Thomas A. "Jonathan Edwards' Conception of the Church." *Church History: Studies in Christianity and Culture,* Vol. 23 (April 1954): 51–66.

———. "Solomon Stoddard and the Theology of Revival." In *A Miscellany of American Christianity: Essays in Honor of H. Shelton Smith,* edited by Stuart C. Henry. Durham: Duke University, 1963.

Shimizu, Tadashige. "The Meaning of Moral Sense in Thomas Jefferson's Political Thought." *The Japanese Journal of Asian Studies,* no. 6 (1995): 67–80.

Shurleff, N. B., Ed. *Records of the Governor and Company of the Massachusetts Bay in New England.* Boston: William White, 1853.

Smith, H. Shelton, Robert T. Handy, and Lefferts A. Loetscher. *American Christianity: An Historical Interpretation with Representative Documents.* New York: Charles Scribner's Sons, 1960.

Stoddard, Solomon. *An Appeal to the Learned. Being a Vindication of the right of Visible Saints to the Lord's Supper, though They Be Destitute of a Saving Work of God's Spirit on Their Hearts; against the Exceptions of Mr. Increase Mather.* Boston: B. Green, 1709.

———. *The Doctrine of Instituted Churches Explained and Proved From the Word of God.* London: 1700.

———. *The Efficacy of the Fear of Hell.* Boston: B. Green, 1713.

———. "Galatians 3:1." In Thomas M., and Virginia L. Davis. *Edward Taylor vs. Solomon Stoddard: The Nature of the Lord's Supper.* Boston: Twayne Publishers, 1981: 129–147.

———. "The Gospel is the Means of Conversion." In *The Puritan Pulpit – The American Puritans: Solomon Stoddard.* Edited by Don Kistler. Orlando: Soli Deo Gloria Publications, 2005: 25–45.

———. *A Guide to Christ or the Way of Directing Souls that are under the Work of Conversion.* Morgan: Soli Deo Gloria Publications, 1998.

———. *The Inexcusableness of Neglecting the Worship of God.* Boston: B. Green, 1708.

———. *The Nature of Saving Conversion.* Morgan: Soli Deo Gloria, 1999.

———. *The Safety of Appearing at the Day of Judgment; In the Righteousness of Christ, Opened and Applied.* Northampton: Thomas M. Pomroy, 1804.

———. "Sermon 2: To Preach the Gospel to the Poor," Appendix to *A Guide to Christ.* Morgan: Soli Deo Gloria Publications, 1998: 85–99.

———. *Three Sermons Lately Preached at Boston.* Boston: B. Green, 1717.

———. *A Treatise Concerning Conversion.* Boston: James Franklin, 1719.

Stoddard, William Leavitt. "A Liberal Among the Puritans," microfilm reel no. 24, *The Judd Manuscript.* Forbes Library, Northampton, MA.

Stout, Harry S. *The New England Soul: Preaching and Religious Culture in Colonial New England.* New York: Oxford University, 1986.

Sweeney, Douglas A. *Jonathan Edwards and the Ministry of the Word.* Downers Grove: InterVarsity, 2009.

Sweeney, Kevin. "River Gods and Related Minor Deities: The Williams Family and the Connecticut Valley, 1637–1790." PhD diss., Yale University, 1986.

Tarbox, I. N. "Jonathan Edwards as a Man and the Ministers of the Last Century." *The New Englander* xxxxiii (1884): 620–640.

Taylor, Edward. *Edward Taylor's "Church Records" and Related Sermons.* Edited by Norman Grabo. East Lansing: Michigan State University, 1966.

———. *Treatise Concerning the Lord's Supper (1694).* Edited by Norman Grabo. East Lansing: Michigan State University, 1966.

Tipson, Baird. "The Judgment of Charity in the Early New England Churches." *Church History* 44 (1975).

Trumbull, James Russell. *The History of Northampton from its Settlement in 1654.* Northampton: Gazette Printing Co, 1898.

Vaughan, Alden T. *The Puritan Tradition in America, 1620–1730.* Hanover: University Press of New England, 1972.

Walker, Williston. *The Creeds and Platforms of Congregationalism.* Boston: Charles Scribner's, 1969.

Walsh, James P. "The Great Awakening in the First Congregational Church of Woodbury, Connecticut." *The William and Mary Quarterly* 28, (Oct 1971): 543–562.

———. "Solomon Stoddard's Open Communion: A Reexamination." *The New England Quarterly* 43, (March 1970): 97–114.

White, C. E. "Were Hooker and Shepherd Closet Arminians?" *Calvin Theological Journal* 20, (April 1985): 33–42.

Whitefield, George. *George Whitefield's Journals.* Edinburgh: Banner of Truth, 1978.

Williams, William. *Death of a Prophet Lamented and Improved.* Boston: Green, 1729.

Ziff, Larzer. *The Career of John Cotton: Puritanism and the American Experience.* Princeton: Princeton University, 1962.

———. *Puritanism in America: New Culture in a New World.* New York: Viking Press, 1973.

# Online Resources

Bremer, Francis. "Congregations before Congregationalism: Social and Spiritual Roots of Cambridge Platform." *United Church of Christ* (1998). No pages. Online: http://www.ucc.org/beliefs/theology/congregations-before.html.

Calvin, John. "Institutes of the Christian Religion, Inst. 4:16 – Infant Baptism." *A Puritan's Mind* (2009). No pages. Online: http://www.apuritansmind.com/covenant-theology/dr-john-calvin-on-infant-baptism/.

"Cambridge Platform." *The History of American Thought* (2002). No pages. Online: www.americanphilosophy.net/cambridge_platform.htm.

"English Dissenters: Brownists." *Ex Libris.org* (1997-2008). No pages. Online: http://www.exlibris.org/nonconform/engdis/brownists.html.

Foxcroft, Thomas. "Being a Letter to the Author . . . " *Jonathan Edwards [1737] Ecclesiastical Writings.* Edited by David D. Hall. Vol. 12. 327–349. WJE Online

"Historic Highlights." *Historic Northampton* (2010). No pages. Online: http://www.historic-northampton.org/highlights/brief.html.

McClendon, John. "Puritan Jurisprudence: Progress and Inconsistency," *Center for Reformed Theology and Apologetics* (1990). No pages. Online: http://www.reformed.org/webfiles/antithesis/index.html?mainframe=/webfiles/antithesis/v1n1/ant_v1n1_juris.html#fn20.

Murdy, Peter. "The Cambridge Platform." *Pilgrim Platform* (1998). Online: http://pilgrim-platform.org/the-cambridge-platform/.

Ross, Phillip A. "Half-Way Covenant." No pages. Online: http://pilgrim-platform.org/2010/halfway-covenant/.

Tracy, Patricia J. "American National Biography: Solomon Stoddard." *Pragmatism.org* (2000). No pages. Online: http://www.americanphilosophy.net/stoddard_bio.htm.

"Westminster Confession of Faith." Chapter III; Article V. *Center for Reformed Theology and Apologetics,* (1996-2009). No pages. Online: http://www.reformed.org/documents/wcf_with_proofs/index.html?foot=/documents/wcf_with_proofs/III_fn.html#fn8.